THE

OLTL **one life to live**

40TH ANNIVERSARY
TRIVIA BOOK

THE
OLTL one life to live
40TH ANNIVERSARY TRIVIA BOOK

A Fun, Fact-Filled, Everything-You-Want-to-Know Guide to Your Favorite Soap!

Gerry Waggett

HYPERION

NEW YORK

Library of Congress Cataloging-in-Publication Data

Waggett, Gerard J.
   The one life to live 40th anniversary trivia book : a fun, fact-filled, everything-you-want-to-know guide to your favorite soap! / by Gerry Waggett.
        p.   cm.
      Includes bibliographical references.
      ISBN 978-1-4013-2309-7
   1. One life to live (Television program)—Miscellanea. I.Title.
      PN1992.77.O48W34 2008
      791.45'72—dc22   2008009649

Hyperion books are available for special promotions, premiums, or corporate training. For details contact Michael Rentas, Proprietary Markets, Hyperion, 77 West 66th Street, 12th floor, New York, New York 10023, or call 212-456-0133.

Book design by Renato Stanisic

FIRST EDITION

10 9 8 7 6 5 4 3 2 1

For my nieces,
Taylor, Norma, and Ava
and my nephew,
Matthew

Contents

Acknowledgments

I need to thank my editor Gretchen Young, who agreed that *One Life to Live*'s Fortieth Anniversary merited a book and believed that I was the one to write it. You will always be my favorite of the show's myriad guest stars.

For taking care of so many problems, big and small, I am indebted to Sarah Mandell and Elizabeth Sabo.

On a personal note, I must thank my parents, Barbara and Fred Waggett, for their continued support throughout the years. For their contributions to my career I also need to thank my aunt Margaret Connolly; my uncle Ed Connolly; my brothers, Michael, Kevin, and Freddie; my nieces, Taylor, Ava, and Norma; my nephew, Matthew; and my sister-in-law, Christine.

In addition to my family, my friends have played pivotal roles not only in my life but also in my career: Chris Farrell; Jerry Stonehouse; Jim McCarthy; Keri O'Brien; Robin Di-Carlo; Jim and Christina Burke and Brady; the Walshes (Jamie, Mike, Connie, Brigitte, Brendan, and Marita); Janet, Brian, and Lauren Blanchard; Stacey Impellizziere;

Mackey Crowley (a relatively new but completely devoted *One Life to Live* fan); Scott Reedy (a great resource and sounding board for all things soap operatic); Don Casali; Mike Dubson; Dr. John Ferrante; Lynda Hirsch; Joanna Hussey; Coni, John, and Hardy Martucci; Amanda Richards; Louise Shaffer; Janet Tavares; and Katie Brown and her staff at the Adams Street Library.

Introduction

In 1982, Kristen Meadows, who played Asa Buchanan's (Phil Carey) cheerleader mistress Mimi King on *One Life to Live*, did a personal appearance at Jordan Marsh, a department store in downtown Boston. Although it meant missing an episode of *One Life to Live* (and maybe a class or two), I could not give up the chance to meet an actress from the show. I was still upset that I'd missed seeing *General Hospital*'s Luke and Laura (Tony Geary and Genie Francis) in Harvard Yard the year before. Not only did I get a place at the front of the line to see Kristen Meadows, my ticket number was called, winning me a picture taken with her. She was the first soap actress I'd ever met.

I had been watching *One Life to Live* for a little over a year at this point. My habit started with my tuning in to *General Hospital* early each day and growing intrigued by what I was seeing in *OLTL*'s final few minutes. Thinking back, I must have seen minutes of the show here and there when I was a kid tuning in to *Dark Shadows* early. I can remember scenes of a man lying in a hospital bed, his faced all wrapped up in bandages, which might have been Dr. Larry Wolek as the show transitioned from James Storm to his brother Michael. Although I could hardly have gotten away with becoming a soap addict at age six—my father thought I watched too much TV as it was—I really wish I'd seen the show back in those days.

While researching this book, I was reviewing all the great story lines, appreciating them not only for their content but also for their place in television history. I have always listed Clara Gray/Carla Benari's (Ellen Holly) deception, passing herself off as white, as the one soap opera story line I most regret never having seen. The story line was already controversial when black doctor Price Trainor (Peter DeAnda, Thurman Scott) kissed his (presumably) white patient. But then, to be thrown that curve, that Carla was black herself—I cannot imagine a bigger shock for the audience watching.

Thanks to the late nineties miniseries *A Daytime to Remember*, I did finally get to see Karen Wolek's (Judith Light) big courtroom confession: "How much more do you want, Mr. Callison? Haven't I said what everyone wants to hear? What you want everyone to hear? That I am a common hooker . . ." As great a moment as that was, I would pay good money to see the whole story line that led up to that climax.

As much as I regret missing Carla's passing for white and Karen's descent into prostitution, I consider myself lucky to have started watching when I did, to have caught all the great story lines from the past three decades.

My favorites, in chronological order . . .

Dr. Ivan Kipling's Obsession with Karen

As Ivan Kipling, the highly respected neurosurgeon who frequented prostitutes, Jack Betts turned in one of the most fascinating performances in the show's history. Afraid of Karen Wolek because she knew all about his dark desires, Ivan threw her down a flight of stairs, then was assigned to her case when she was admitted to the hospital. The not so good doctor fluctuated between his Hippocratic oath and his need to kill this woman. When Karen awoke, unable to move or speak, staring at the man who had tried to kill her, Judith Light's eyes captured Karen's terror. Ivan's return visit to town years later, when he was implanting mind-controlling devices into Larry Wolek and Ed Hall's (Al Freeman, Jr.) brains to get to Karen, whom he now loved, lacked the edge of their first interplay, but Betts and Light made it work.

Asa Buchanan Romances Sam Vernon

Of all Asa's love stories, his pursuit of Samantha Vernon (Julie Montgomery, Dorian LoPinto) remains my favorite. I loved Asa's combination of grand gestures (his Hamptons barbecue for Sam's birthday party) and devious scheming (making sure that Sam walked in on her boyfriend Mick Gordon [James McDonnell] making out with Tina Clayton [Andrea Evans]). Adding a Gothic touch to the grand romance was Nicole Bonnard (Taina Elg), the mysterious Frenchwoman who turned out to be Asa's supposedly dead first wife, Olympia. From Olympia's attempt to shoot Asa at the wedding to her stunning appearance at the masquerade party in Asa's new mansion on a rainy night, this was storytelling on a grand scale—just like Asa himself.

Jenny's Baby Switch

One of my all-time favorite *OLTL* actresses is Brynn
Thayer, who played ex-nun Jenny Wolek. Of all her story
lines, nothing packed the punch of Jenny's discovering that
her daughter Mary really belonged to ex-prostitute Katrina
Karr (Nancy Snyder) and that her own daughter had died
at birth. (Jenny's sister Karen had switched the babies in
the nursery, believing that Katrina Karr didn't want her
child.) From Jenny's realization of the truth to the moment
she handed Mary over to Katrina—nothing in the show's
history broke your heart into smaller pieces.

The Return of Niki Smith

Viki's alternate personality had been alluded to often enough
that I wanted to see actress Erika Slezak transform from the
stately Viki into trashy Niki. And what a transformation.
Slezak's mastery with the dual role established her as the best
actress on daytime. The tightly plotted story encompassed
not only Viki's mental battles but the revelation that Victor
Lord was Tina Clayton's father, the machinations of Tina's
villainous boyfriend Mitch Laurence (played with demonic
malevolence by Roscoe Born), and the murder of Harry
O'Neill (Frank Converse), blamed on Tina and witnessed
only by Niki Smith, who promptly receded into Viki's mind.

Homophobia in Llanview

While most soap operas plug their teen characters into
simple love triangles and silly adventures, head writer Michael Malone handed his teen actors the heavy lifting in a
story line tackling homophobia. As gay teen Billy Douglas,

Ryan Phillippe avoided the easy stereotypes without losing the character's emotional depth. When Billy cried while coming out, nothing about those tears felt girlish. As Reverend Carpenter, the minister falsely accused of molesting Billy, Wortham Krimmer was a paragon of quiet strength. The climax, filmed at an actual display of the AIDS quilt, underscored the need for this story line to be told.

Marty's Gang Rape

As Marty Saybrooke, a former party girl who is gang raped at a fraternity party, Susan Haskell turned in an amazingly painful performance. From Marty's feelings of disgust, to fear, to anger, to her quest for justice, Haskell did not miss one beat that this story needed. Marty's testimony during the rape trial ranks up there with Karen Wolek's admission to being a prostitute. The story line also pushed Todd Manning (then played by Roger Howarth) onto the list of *OLTL*'s all-time most despicable villains.

Viki's Ultimate Battle with DID

As great as Erika Slezak was in 1985, playing Viki and Niki, the woman outdid herself when Viki's other five personalities emerged. Slezak tackled playing everything from an angry young boy to a shattered little girl to a maniac arsonist to her own father who molested her. Slezak would have deserved all six Emmys she's won just for this one story line. As if playing the alters were not enough, Slezak also tackled Viki's most emotionally wrenching material as she remembered that her father had sexually abused her and realized that one of her alters had murdered him.

"Babes Behind Bars"

Usually, I'm not a fan of musical episodes, but when you have talents like Kassie DePaiva (Blair Cramer) and Catherine Hickland (Lindsay Rappaport), it would be a sin not to hand them a microphone once in a while. This episode, shown on the Fourth of July, offered a fun break from the norm and featured Kassie DePaiva in prison stripes belting out a version of "I'll Never Fall in Love Again" that could have been released as a single.

Todd and Blair

Now on their fifth wedding, Todd Manning (Roger Howarth, Trevor St. John) and Blair Cramer (Kassie DePaiva) are day-

Blair and Todd Manning (Kassie DePaiva and Trevor St. John)

time's most twisted yet compelling couple to watch. They hurt each other in the most horrible ways, but completely consistent with their scarred personalities. In a very real sense, Todd and Blair are the perfect soap opera couple because they will never settle into the happiness that has dulled the passion for so many other supercouples.

The Killing Club Mystery

As far as murder mysteries on daytime go, this offered up some unexpected twists: We immediately suspected Marcie Walsh's (Kathy Brier) obnoxious publicist, then dismissed him once the police investigated him and validated his alibi for one of the murders. We didn't suspect an accomplice until later on. The mystery also offered its share of fun death traps, among them seeing Natalie Buchanan (Melissa Archer) buried alive in a cheerleader's uniform.

My affection for the Killing Club Mystery is highly personal. The book on which the murders were based was actually published by Hyperion, my publisher, and edited by Gretchen Young, my editor, who popped up at Marcie Walsh's book launch party. (I'd never seen what Gretchen looked like until that episode.) While meeting Kristen Meadows back in 1982 placed me within six degrees of separation from every actor who has ever worked on *One Life to Live,* even more impressive to me, working with the same editor as Marcie Walsh has placed me within those same six degrees to every *character* who has ever set foot in Llanview.

First Impressions

In 1968, *One Life to Live* debuted with the image of a roaring fireplace. Those flames would have looked even more ominous had the show been allowed to keep its original title, *Between Heaven and Hell.*

Since then, the show has changed its title sequences numerous times:

1975: A mountain sunrise replaced the fireplace.
1980: The mountain sunrise was expanded to include even more nature imagery, birds and clouds, while the show delved deeper into the darker side of urban living, such as political corruption and organized crime.
1984: Faces were added to the opening as black-and-white head shots of the cast were superimposed over scenes from around Llanview. Cast changes necessitated these credits being updated several times a year.
1987: Lyrics, sung by Peabo Bryson, were added to the

theme music, making *One Life to Live* one of very few soaps to have a theme song with words.

1992: Cast faces were dispensed with in favor of such romantic images as a champagne bottle, a newborn baby, and satin sheets flapping in the wind.

1995: The faces returned, this time intercut with urban scenes of factories and subway trains that truly captured the fact that Llanview was a city, quite distinct from the quaint village feel of *All My Children*'s Pine Valley. While the size of the cast did not allow for everyone to be seen each day, half the cast was shown one day, half the other, with Erika Slezak being the exception; her image was used at the end of every day's opening credits.

2004: All three ABC soap operas (*All My Children, One Life to Live,* and *General Hospital*) revamped their title sequences as part of a grand plan to unify the daytime canvas. Cast members were now shown against a black background.

1

40 Years to *Life*

*Milestones and News Items from
the First Four Decades*

1967

During the 1950s and '60s, CBS dominated daytime with hits like *As the World Turns, The Guiding Light,* and *Search for Tomorrow.* One of the very few non-CBS soaps to be thriving was NBC's *Another World,* whose popularity was attributed to then head writer Agnes Nixon (a former writer for *As the World Turns* and *Guiding Light*). Nixon had been credited with saving *Another World* from cancellation. ABC, which had only two successful soap operas at the time (*General Hospital* and the cult hit *Dark Shadows*) approached Nixon to create a new soap opera, which would be scheduled between those two shows. At home, in a desk drawer, Nixon had filed away the bible for *All My Children,* which, several years before, Procter & Gamble had declined to produce. Having lost faith in *All My Children* because of that rejection,[1] Nixon set about creating a brand-new soap opera.

1968

Agnes Nixon intended to title her new show *Between Heaven and Hell*. Religion would be playing a role in the lives of the varied characters, which included an Irish Catholic and a Jewish family. While the title captured the darker, edgier feel of late afternoon soaps like *Dark Shadows* and *The Edge of Night,* sponsors found the title a bit too controversial. Nixon compromised with *One Life to Live,* an ironic title given the fact that its signature story line, Victoria Lord's (then Gillian Spencer) multiple personality disorder, revolved around a woman literally leading a double life.

On July 15, *One Life to Live* debuted on ABC in the 3:30 time slot, nestled between *General Hospital* and *Dark Shadows.* Agnes Nixon prided herself on the show's ethnic and economic diversity. The four core families would be the blue collar and Polish Woleks, the Irish Catholic Rileys, the very upper-class Lords, and the Jewish Siegels. In an article that appeared in *The New York Times* shortly before the show debuted, Nixon emphasized the fact that the show would be featuring black actors in prominent story lines, a feat being done almost nowhere else on television. The character of Sadie Gray, an African-American (played by Tony winner Lillian Hayman), held down a prominent job, heading up the housekeeping department in the hospital. As with the best of soap opera characters, references were made to some secret involving Sadie's long absent daughter.

The first episode began with the death of Dr. Ted Hale (Terry Logan). Dr. Hale had fallen down a flight of stairs at the hospital during an argument with Dr. Larry Wolek (originated by Paul Tulley), who would be charged with murder. Dr. Ted would not be the last character to die falling down those stairs, nor would this be the last time that Larry Wolek would be charged with murder.

Several months into the run, the show introduced "a new character"—Niki Smith. Flashy, trashy Niki Smith was actually an alternate personality of the very proper Victoria Lord, older daughter in the town's leading family. While the characters Niki encountered thought that she looked like Viki, no one realized the truth. The split personality allowed for an unusual love triangle, especially for its day: Viki Lord was in love with fellow reporter Joe Riley (Lee Patterson) while Niki Smith was taking up with Joe's best friend, truck driver Vince Wolek (originated by Anthony Ponzini). Although Viki would be "cured" a year later, the Niki Smith personality still breaks out on occasion, forty years later.

1969

While the Joe/Viki/Niki/Vince love triangle was one of daytime's most unusual, the Jim Craig/Carla Benari/Price Trainor was its most controversial. Dr. Jim Craig (Robert Milli, Nat Polen) had fallen in love with Carla Benari (Ellen Holly), a beautiful actress he was treating for cirrhosis of the liver. When Dr. Price Trainor (Peter DeAnda, Thurman Scott) took over as Carla's doctor, he too fell in love with her. The doctor/patient boundary was not the issue. The real powder keg: Price Trainor was black. When he and Carla finally gave in to their mutual attraction and kissed, ABC was flooded with calls of protest. Fans didn't want to see a black man kissing a white woman. An ABC affiliate in Texas dropped the show from its afternoon schedule solely because of that kiss. While the love triangle *was* interracial, it wasn't so in the way that the fans had been led to believe. Carla, as it turned out, was not white; she was black. She was the mystery daughter Sadie Gray had been missing for so many years. Therefore, Carla's romance with Dr. Jim Craig had been the interracial relationship. Carla's story line as a light-skinned black woman posing as white was considered the most controversial story line daytime had seen up to that point.

During the show's first year on the air, viewers saw three different Larry Woleks. Paul Tulley originated the role and was shortly replaced by James Storm, who only intended to stick around for a few months himself. As he was preparing to leave, he recommended a replacement: his younger brother Michael, who was living in California at the time. James Storm's last scenes on the show found Larry falling asleep in a storeroom right before a fire broke out. For weeks, Larry lay in a hospital bed, his burned face completely bandaged. When the bandages were finally removed, viewers got their first glimpse of Michael Storm as Larry. Although Larry was recast twice that first year, Michael Storm stayed with the show for more than thirty years.

1970

In response to a request from the White House asking the entertainment industry to tackle the growing problem of drug abuse among the nation's young, Agnes Nixon penned a story line that found Dr. Jim Craig's troubled daughter Cathy Craig (then played by Amy Levitt) becoming an addict. To drive home the point that addiction was a real-life problem and not merely a story line, the show taped Cathy's rehabilitation scenes at Odyssey House, a real treatment center in New York City. There, Nat Polen and Levitt filmed the group therapy scenes not with actors but with the actual counselors and recovering addicts.

1971

Erika Slezak began her run as Victoria Lord Davidson. She was hired to take over the role the very same day that she auditioned in front of the show's creator, Agnes Nixon. Slezak was also asked to start the very next day. The thirty-seven years that have passed since that first day have not only earned Slezak a record-setting six Best Actress Emmys, those years also make her the longest-running cast member on the show and her performance one of the longest running in daytime history.

1972

The writers tackled the issue of postpartum depression through the character of Viki's sister Meredith Lord Wolek (Lynn Benesch). One of the twins Meredith had been carrying was stillborn. Adding to her grief, the doctors warned her that she could never risk getting pregnant again. The situation triggered a deep depression. Just as the show had incorporated scenes from Odyssey House to emphasize that drug abuse was a real problem in the world, the producers hoped to call attention to the issue of postpartum depression as a legitimate medical concern for new mothers by bringing in a real-life psychiatrist, one TV audiences would recognize and trust, to treat Meredith—Dr. Joyce Brothers.

The character of Cathy Craig (now played by Dorrie Kavanaugh), who had been the center of 1970's Odyssey House story line, had gotten a job at *The Banner,* Llanview's leading newspaper. Cathy wrote a well-received article on venereal disease, an article that was not only read by the residents of Llanview but available to the general public as well. Anyone who wrote into the show requesting Cathy's article was mailed a copy, which had actually been penned by show creator Agnes Nixon. That same year, Nixon wrote an article for *The New York Times* defending soap operas.

1973

Agnes Nixon, who had been cowriting the show since the very beginning, stepped down, leaving it entirely in the hands of Gordon Russell. Nixon left to concentrate her efforts on *All My Children*. While not actively cowriting *OLTL* any longer, Nixon did stay on in a consulting capacity.

1974

Second only to Viki's battles with disassociative personality disorder, the feud between Dr. Dorian Cramer Lord and Viki Lord Davidson remains the show's longest-running story line. Seeds for the feud were planted with the accidental overdose of cancer patient Rachel Wilson (Nancy Barrett). Dorian (then played by Nancy Pinkerton) and her lover, Dr. Mark Toland (Tommy Lee Jones), had both administered potassium chloride to Rachel, then let Larry Wolek be blamed for their mistake, for which he was sent to prison. When the truth came out, Larry's close friend and one-time sister-in-law Viki used her position as a hospital board member to have Dorian suspended. Dorian retaliated by accepting a position as in-house doctor for Viki's heart patient father, Victor Lord. While cooled at times through the years, the feud continues to this day.

Nixon sold Creative Horizons, the company that had been producing *One Life to Live* as well as *All My Children*, to ABC, giving the network even greater control over the two shows.

1975

Among the most popular story lines on *Another World* had been a love triangle involving heroine Alice Matthews (Jacqueline Courtney), self-made businessman Steve Frame (George Reinholt), and the ever-scheming gold digger Rachel Davis (a role originated by Robin Strasser). When Courtney and Reinholt were fired, *OLTL* producers saw a chance to grab a percentage of *Another World*'s audience. Courtney and Reinholt were quickly hired to play Pat Ashley and Viki's long-lost brother Tony Harris. Allowing the show to jump right into the Tony/Pat romance, the characters' backstory included a previous relationship down in South America some ten years prior. At the time, the producers had also offered Strasser the role of Cathy Craig, intending to re-create—at least visually—one of daytime's most popular love triangles. Strasser, who had left *Another World* in the early seventies, turned down the offer when she realized that the show was intending to let another actress go to give the role to her.[2] Lightning, however, did not strike twice for Courtney and Reinholt, who failed to click as Pat and Tony.

1976

In June, the character of Victor Lord (played at this point by Shepperd Strudwick) died as a combination of two strokes and his wife Dorian's refusal to give him the medicine he needed. Most significant about Victor Lord's murder has been the way future writers have revised the facts of his life and death to generate story line. In the late 1980s, viewers discovered that he had been more than a domineering father and businessman; he was a power-crazed madman who had built his own underground city. Several years later, his memory was further disgraced by the revelation that he was a child molester who had been sexually abusing his own daughter Viki. In 1995, nearly twenty years after Victor's death, the audience would discover that Tori, one of Viki Buchanan's alternate personalities, had actually smothered her father with a pillow while he lay in his hospital bed. In 2003, nearly twenty-seven years after Victor Lord's death, the audience would learn that the man was actually still alive. While soap operas commonly bring characters back from the dead, at twenty-six years, Victor Lord holds the record for the longest time span between on-screen death and subsequent resurrection.

By the mid-1970s, *One Life to Live*'s lead-in, *General Hospital*, had begun to slide in the ratings up against CBS's megapopular celebrity game show *Match Game*. While *All My Children*, ABC's then top-rated soap, had expanded to an hour, the network decided to experiment with both *One Life* and *GH*'s time slots by expanding the two soap operas to forty-five minutes each, creating an hour-and-a-half time block. Viewers, the network reasoned, were not going to switch channels two-thirds of the way through a show. Nor, ABC executives hoped, would these viewers then flip over to *Match Game* halfway through. Because *One Life* had been climbing in the ratings, the order was flipped around, making *OLTL* the lead-in to *General Hospital*.

GH and *One Life to Live* remain the only two soap operas to have aired at the forty-five-minute length.

1977

The reformed hooker became a staple of daytime soaps during the 1970s. On shows like *The Young and the Restless* and *All My Children,* the hero would rescue the prostitute from life on the street and then fall in love with her. Through the character of Larry Wolek's new bride Karen, *One Life to Live* reversed that formula, exploring what lured a woman into that world. Bored with being a housewife and hungry for the finer things in life, Karen began sleeping with men in exchange for money and expensive gifts. 1977 also marked the year that Judith Light took over the role of Karen.

Through Karen, the character of con artist/blackmailer/pimp Marco Dane was introduced. Marco had been romantically involved with Karen in a commune and came to town to squeeze some money out of his old lover. Played by Gerald Anthony, Marco became the show's umbrella villain, preying upon the majority of Llanview's residents, blackmailing even Viki. By the 1980s, despite Marco's rap sheet, the character had been remolded into the show's leading anti-hero and often its comic relief.

The death of Naomi Vernon (Teri Keane) ventured into territory where soap operas still rarely go—suicide. Fearing that she was losing her husband Will (Anthony George) to a younger woman, their son Brad's (Jameson Parker) girlfriend Jenny (Katherine Glass), Naomi swallowed a handful of pills. While Naomi expected her son Brad home in time to find her, save her life, and let his father know what had happened, her scheme didn't play out according to plan. She may not have intended to do so, but Naomi did kill herself, making her one of the very few soap opera characters to die by suicide. (Note: Brad didn't make it home in time to save his mother's life because he was having sex with Lana Mc-Clain [Jacklyn Zeman], who herself would die of an accidental overdose a few months later also because of Brad, who unwittingly handed his already drunken lover a sleeping pill–spiked glass of milk.)

1978

On January 16, the show expanded to an hour—as did *General Hospital*. The beginning time was moved up half an hour to 2:00, where it has stayed for the last thirty years. The writers certainly upped the drama level during the first week of hour-long shows, focusing around the death of Pat Ashley's son Brian (Stephen Austin), who had been hit by Talbot Huddleston's (Byron Sanders) car. Brian had run out into the street when he discovered that his real father was Tony Lord. The death gave actress Jacqueline Courtney some of her most powerful material and Karen Wolek another secret to hide: She had been in the car with Talbot.

With so many soap operas like *All My Children* and *The Young and the Restless* focusing on younger, sexually active characters, *One Life to Live* introduced sixteen-year-old Tina Lord, played by Andrea Evans. Tina's mother, Irene, who was dying, had requested that her best friend Viki raise Tina. (Neither Viki nor Tina nor the audience nor even the writers at the time realized that Tina was actually Viki's half-sister.) In a daringly seedy story line that brushed along the lines of child pornography, Marco Dane was blackmailing Viki with photos of a naked Tina. So as not to make Marco (whom the producers wanted to keep around) a true child pornographer, he had not actually taken nude photos of Tina, just superimposed her head on top of other naked bodies, presumably ones belonging to women of consenting age.

1979

During Marco Dane's murder trial, Victoria Lord Riley sat accused of committing the crime. In an effort to exonerate her good friend, Karen Wolek took the stand with the intention of naming her ex-john Talbot Huddleston as the real killer. Under cross-examination, Karen broke down and admitted that for the previous two years, she had been working as a prostitute. The testimony earned Light an Emmy and the scene a place in daytime history. *TV Guide* once ranked Karen's testimony as one of the 100 Most Memorable Moments in TV History.

Joe Riley's deaths bookended the decade. Joe had been presumed killed in a car accident in 1970 and did not resurface for two years. This time, he died from a brain tumor—but not before picking out his replacement both as editor of *The Banner* and as Viki's next husband: cowboy Clint Buchanan (Clint Ritchie).

1980

The phenomenal success of the primetime soap opera *Dallas* did not go unnoticed by daytime. NBC was spinning off the similarly titled *Texas* from its well-established *Another World*. Beating NBC to the punch, *One Life to Live* brought Texas to Pennsylvania, introducing Clint Buchanan's oil-rich father Asa (Phil Carey) and brother Bo (Robert S. Woods). When Woods landed the role of Bo, he called up his good friend Steve Kanaly (Ray Krebbs, *Dallas*) to tell him, "I'm going to be the Ray Krebbs of daytime."[3] Carey doubted that the *OLTL* audience would accept the Buchanans.[4] Not only did the fans accept them, within a few years, the Buchanans would become the show's core family, helped along through its merger with the already established Lords via Clint's marriage to Viki.

Robert S. Woods and Jacqueline Courtney (Pat Ashley) traveled to Paris for the show's first overseas remote. Throughout the decade the show would travel all over the world (Venice, Austria, Brazil, the Caribbean), usually as a backdrop to some tale of action/adventure. The focus of this remote, however, was much quieter, mainly romance. Even more remarkable, the Paris remote involved only two main characters, one of whom (Bo Buchanan) had been on the show for less than a year. The Paris remote served two purposes. One was to kick into high gear the romance between Bo and Pat, whom the producers hoped would become the show's new supercouple. (They fizzled.) The Paris remote also introduced mystery woman Nicole Bonnard, who would turn out to be Bo's presumed dead mother. Her big secret, that Bo was not Asa's biological son, turned out to be a lie.

1981

The phenomenal rise in popularity of *General Hospital* lifted ratings all across daytime, but no soap opera benefited more than *One Life to Live,* which climbed all the way to number two among the soaps, thanks to *GH* viewers tuning in early and getting hooked on what they saw.

The year ended with Asa's masquerade ball, where his first wife Olympia (aka Nicole Bonnard) finally revealed that she was not dead. The party, which lasted one night in Llanview time, took three weeks to tape and played out over the course of an entire month.

1982

General Hospital became an industry phenomenon thanks not only to the intense popularity of Luke and Laura, but also to the incorporation of mob warfare, espionage, and science fiction, which was credited with bringing younger male viewers to the show. In one of daytime's most memorable story lines, "The Ice Princess," Port Charles was literally frozen in the summer with a weather-controlling device. *One Life to Live* was one of the many soaps that subsequently tried their hands at science fiction. Dr. Ivan Kipling (Jack Betts), the brilliant neurologist with a fetish for prostitutes, absent from town since he tried to kill ex-hooker Karen Wolek, was reintroduced and reinvented as a mad scientist implanting mind-control devices inside the heads of Larry Wolek (Michael Storm) and Ed Hall. (When he resurfaced in the mid-1980s, Dr. Kipling would be sporting a bionic hand.) Also brought back at this same time, Viki's brother Tony (now played by Chip Lucia) was involved with the discovery of an alternate energy source for fueling race cars.

1983

Ernest Graves, who originated the role of Victor Lord, and Shepperd Strudwick, who succeeded him, both passed away within a few months of each other; Strudwick in mid-January, Graves in early June.

1984

Paul Rauch, who had been executive producing *Another World* since 1972, replaced Jean Arley as executive producer. One of daytime's most powerful producers, Rauch had once convinced Procter & Gamble, which owned *Another World*, and NBC to extend the soap opera to an unprecedented ninety minutes a day. When Rauch joined *OLTL*, the network was tired of the show imitating *General Hospital*. Instead, ABC wanted the sort of realism that had been *Another World*'s hallmark during the 1970s. Strong-willed, Rauch ignored the request for realism and set out to outdo *General Hospital* with outlandish story lines and science fiction adventures beyond anything *GH* had done. (Of course, this was before *GH* dropped an alien from outer space into the middle of town.)

ABC considered giving all their daytime soap operas a hiatus during the Summer Olympics but feared losing audience members to the other networks. Instead, only ABC's two lowest rated soaps, *Ryan's Hope* and *Loving*, were shelved for the two weeks. *One Life to Live*, along with *All My Children* and *General Hospital*, was reduced to forty minutes a day.

1985

In an effort to lure back old fans, the show offered them the return of Niki Smith, Victoria Lord Riley's alternate personality, which had not been seen in fifteen years. Prior to this return, Erika Slezak herself had taped only a handful of Niki scenes, which had been used as pseudo-flashbacks. By the time Slezak took over the role of Viki, the character had been supposedly "cured" of her split personality (as it was then called). Niki's return was triggered by the discovery that the recently returned Tina Lord was her half-sister and that Viki had once walked in on her father having sex with Tina's mother. (The real truth lay another eight years in the future.) Slezak herself rose to the challenge, portraying not only Viki and Niki but Niki pretending to be Viki. So powerful was Slezak's performance that the audience would not be waiting another fifteen years to see Niki again.

1986

Uta Hagen's Daytime Emmy nomination for Best Supporting Actress sparked outrage. Hagen had played Hortense, a con artist who faked having "priceless" jewelry stolen from the Vernon Inn on *One Life to Live*. The role, a guest spot, had lasted only one week. Hagen, a then two-time Tony Award winner (*The Country Girl*, *Who's Afraid of Virginia Woolf?*), was also famed for her acting school in Greenwich Village, where many daytimers had studied at one point in their careers. Industry experts theorized that Hagen was nominated based not so much on her performance but on her reputation. The Daytime Emmys reviewed the incident and laid down guidelines determining what constituted a guest spot and what constituted supporting character status. The following year, the Daytime Emmys also created a special category for guest stars, but that lasted only one year. Hagen, it should be noted, did not win the award.

Janet Jackson's breakthrough single "What Have You Done for Me Lately" placed the title *One Life to Live* into heavy rotation on MTV and top 40 radio. The lyrics—written by Jackson and her producers, Jimmy Jam and Terry Lewis—include the line "Soap opera says you've only got one life to live." The song climbed to number four on the pop charts and all the way to number one on the R&B charts.

1987

In possibly the most loved—and hated—story line under Paul Rauch's regime, maybe in the show's entire history, Viki experienced an out-of-body experience during brain surgery and literally floated up to Heaven. In Rauch's view of Heaven, which many critics likened to a spaceship, everyone wore white robes. Among the loved ones with whom Viki reconnected was her late husband, Joe Riley. Since Lee Patterson, who played Joe, had recently returned to the show as Joe's twin brother, Tom, having him play the role of Viki's late husband was not a problem. While critics attacked the story as campy, Slezak was amazed by how many viewers wrote in, thanking her and the show for offering them hope for life after this one life.[5]

1988

After Viki's trip to Heaven, it was husband Clint's turn to do some traveling—time traveling. Blinded by a gunshot, a stubborn Clint had ridden off on his horse to parts unknown near his Arizona ranch. After being thrown off that horse, Clint awoke able to see again—and one hundred years in the past. There, in Buchanan City, Clint came face-to-face with his ancestor Buck Buchanan, a dead ringer for his father Asa (and also played by Phil Carey); Buck's ranch hand Cody Vasquez looked like Clint's son Cord and was also played by John Loprieno. Clint even met Viki's great-grandmother Ginny, played by Erika Slezak. Slezak loved Ginny because up till that point, she was the very first

Viki (Erika Slezak) reunited with her late husband, Joe Riley (Lee Patterson), during a 1987 trip to Heaven.

character on the show whom the actress had originated. Actor Clint Ritchie, a cowboy at heart, has picked Clint's trip back to the Wild West as his favorite story line.[6]

In between having their characters travel back in time and to a futuristic underground city (see 1989), the writers decided to follow, at least temporarily, the first rule of writing: Write what you know. What they all knew was working on a soap opera, and what they came up with was *Fraternity Row*, *One Life to Live*'s soap-opera-within-a-soap-opera. *Fraternity Row*'s lead actress, Megan Gordon (Jessica Tuck), would eventually be revealed as Viki's long-lost daughter. Existing characters such as Max Holden (James DePaiva) and Mari Lynn Dennison (Tammy Amerson) were hired as actors on the soap, and Bo Buchanan became the executive producer. The soap-within-a-soap allowed the writers to take *One Life*'s audience behind the scenes of a soap and to poke a little fun at the industry itself.

1989

The decade that had included brain implants, an out-of-body experience, and time travel ended with the show's and daytime's most ambitious foray into science fiction to that point. February sweeps trapped Viki, Tina, and numerous other cast members in Eterna, a now abandoned city-of-the-future which had been built by Victor Lord underneath Llantano Mountain. Eterna—with its various caverns, collapsing bridges, and booby-trapped rooms—was modeled after the Indiana Jones movies popular at the time. Eterna was also the most expensive set ever constructed for a daytime soap opera. During the scenes in which Llantano Mountain was being dug up to rescue Viki and the gang, real oil-well diggers were hired to operate real machinery. More than providing a simple action adventure, Eterna also served as the backdrop against which Viki finally learned that Megan Gordon was the daughter taken away from her at birth.

1990

Andrea Evans left the role of Tina because a stalker had become far too familiar with her work schedule.[7] (Evans did not talk about this matter until several years later, when she was profiled for a *48 Hours* exposé on celebrity stalkers.) In addition to sending Evans threatening letters written in his own blood, the stalker had once slashed his wrists and, when taken to the hospital, listed Evans as his next of kin. Terrified, Evans hired armed guards to accompany her to and from the studio. At one point, the stalker broke into the ABC studios intending to kill Evans. Adding to Evans's fears, sitcom actress Rebecca Shaeffer (who played Annie Barnes on *One Life* in the mid-eighties) had been shot to death by a celebrity stalker the previous summer. Evans not only moved from New York to California to get away from the stalker, she also stepped out of the limelight, putting her career into hibernation for the next decade, taking on only small roles in the occasional film. She would return to soaps in the new millennium but, so far, only LA-based ones (*The Bold and the Beautiful* and *Passions*).

The Michael Grande murder mystery merited the cover of *Soap Opera Digest*: Dennis Parlato, who played Michael, was surrounded by suspects Jessica Tuck as Megan Gordon, Joe Lando as Jake Harrison, Robert S. Woods as Bo Buchanan, Michael Palance as Dan Wolek, and Brenda Brock as Brenda McGillis. According to the cover, we were looking at the killer. By the time the issue went to press, the show's writers had changed the story line. While Brenda, who had been drugged by Michael, was intended to be the killer, the murderer turned out to be Roger Gordon (Larry Pine), who had been lying comatose before the murder and throughout the investigation. Roger, it turned out, emerged from his coma just long enough to kill Michael Grande, then headed back to his hospital bed and his coma.

1991

Deciding that *One Life to Live* needed a fresh perspective, ABC looked outside the realm of daytime television for its next executive producer. Linda Gottlieb, who had produced the film *Dirty Dancing,* the surprise hit of 1987, replaced Paul Rauch as executive producer. Just as ABC looked outside daytime for Gottlieb, Gottlieb looked outside the usual lineup of TV names for the show's new head writer. She picked novelist Michael Malone (*Foolscap, Time's Witness*), whose storytelling style and characterizations she likened to Charles Dickens, whose books had originally been published in a serialized format. Together, Gottlieb and Malone refocused *One Life* from the fantastic (time travel and Eterna) to the socially conscious, bringing the show back to its multi-ethnic, issue-driven, and sometimes controversial roots. At first, the pair experimented with short-term story arcs, such as the saga of a battered wife, tangentially linked to main characters, but quickly abandoned that for the more conventional soap opera format.

1992

Among Michael Malone's first major story lines was Megan Gordon's battle with lupus, a battle which ended with her death during the February sweeps. In the three years Jessica Tuck had been playing Megan, the actress and character had built up quite a fan following, making her death one of the show's most remembered and heartbreaking. As Megan lay in her bed, waiting for her husband Jake Harrison to show up, characters like her mother Viki and her doctor, Larry Wolek (Michael Storm), who had delivered her, shared their memories of life in Llanview, shown to the viewers through a series of clips from old episodes. Malone had added the clip element to the story after watching countless episodes in preparation to take over as head writer; he thought that newcomers like himself would love a glimpse into the show's rich history.

Malone's first potentially controversial story line introduced daytime's first gay teen, Billy Douglas, played by future film star Ryan Phillippe. Billy was Joey Buchanan's (Chris McKenna) best friend, but if Malone had been given his own way, Joey would have been the gay teen.[8] Malone thought that the story line would carry more power if the first gay teen came from a core family. The network, however, worried about losing a potential leading man of the future. So Malone compromised and gave Joey a gay best friend. Billy's story line included a rumor of homosexuality and child molestation involving local minister Andrew Carpenter (Wortham Krimmer), who was accused of having a sexual relationship with Billy—a story that predated the wave of true-life sex scandals in the church. The homophobia story line reached its conclusion with the arrival of the AIDS quilt. Just as Agnes Nixon's historic Odyssey House story line had combined footage of real recovering drug addicts with the character of Cathy Craig, the show filmed scenes at an actual AIDS quilt display in the yard of the Church of Christ the King in New Vernon, New Jersey. Alongside the names of real people who had died from the disease, Andrew Carpenter added a panel to the quilt for his late brother. Billy Douglas chose the ceremony as his venue to come out. In order to show the quilt on air, ABC not only made a sizable contribution to the charity, the network also offered to promote the AIDS quilt's Washington, DC, display and to allow members from the charity input on the scripts. The story line won *One Life to Live* its first GLAAD Media Award as Best Daytime Drama.

Real life merged with fiction as the homophobia story line ended at a real ceremony displaying the AIDS quilt.

Roger Howarth debuted on the show. No one could have predicted the way that Howarth would eventually come to dominate *OLTL*. His first day in Llanview, his character didn't even have a name. He was simply Frat Boy #1 in one of the college scenes. Thanks to Howarth's talents and an intense front-burner story line the following year, Todd Manning would become the show's next centerpiece villain and eventually the show's male lead.

1993

While rape had become an all too common plot device on daytime, *One Life to Live* explored the far less dramatized—especially on daytime—issue of gang rape. The story line was inspired by recent news stories about an increase in this sort of sexual assault on college campuses across the country. *TV Guide*'s Michael Logan hailed the move as one that "may be the most daring plot ever attempted on soaps." A drunken Marty Saybrooke (Susan Haskell) passed out at a college party and was subsequently raped by Todd Manning and two of his fraternity brothers. Close-ups of the rapists' faces during the assault, distorted to capture Marty's scared and drunken perspective, rank among the show's most graphic images. Marty's subsequent quest to bring her rapists to justice dominated the show throughout the entire summer. To insure accuracy, social workers were hired to review the scripts. Marty's mistaken accusation naming Kevin Buchanan (Kirk Geiger) as one of her assailants turned the gang rape and court case into an umbrella story line that encompassed the entire cast. During the weeks leading up to the rape, each Monday's episode began with story recaps much like the technique used on serialized primetime dramas. Taking another cue from primetime in the nineties, ABC also employed the crash-bang technique, cutting out the commercial breaks between the end of one show (in this case, *All My Children*) and the beginning of another (*One Life to Live*).

Missing during the rape trial was Kevin's father, Clint Buchanan. That May, actor Clint Ritchie had been severely injured, and nearly killed, when the tractor he was riding upended and flipped over on top of him. While Ritchie recovered from his injuries, Clint's absence from town was explained with a plane crash and an off-screen convalescence.

On August 26, *The New York Times* ran an obituary for *One Life to Live* alumna Margaret Klenck, who had played

Edwina Lewis. According to the death notice, Klenck had legally changed her name to Edwina Lewis. In reality, Margaret Klenck was very much alive—and still is. It was an actress actually named Edwina Lewis who had passed away. Someone at the *Times,* obviously a *One Life to Live* fan, had seen the name Edwina Lewis, remembered the character, and concocted one of the paper's more colorful if inaccurate obituaries. Two days later, a retraction was issued.[9]

1994

Not only had Linda Gottlieb's *Dirty Dancing* been a box office smash, its soundtrack had gone platinum several times over. Gottlieb, who had been incorporating music more noticeably into the show, produced the soundtrack *One Life to Live: The Best of Love,* making *One Life* one of very few soaps to release a soundtrack. Several artists whose music was featured performed on the show, among them: country star Billy Dean, Darlene Love, and Righteous Brother Bill Medley, who had scored a number one hit with the *Dirty Dancing* theme song "(I've Had) The Time of My Life" (with Jennifer Warnes). The Valentine's Day episode that year heavily featured music from the CD, downplaying the dialogue.

Much like Roseanne herself, her sitcom counterpart, Roseanne Connor was a fan of *One Life to Live.* While dozing off watching the show during the season's penultimate episode, titled "Isn't It Romantic?," Roseanne dreamed of being romanced by Buchanans Bo (Robert S. Woods), Clint (Clint Ritchie), and Cord (John Loprieno). Roseanne had also hoped to include Phil Carey in the fantasy sequence, but those plans didn't pan out. Earlier in the year,

General Hospital's Tony Geary and Genie Francis popped up in character in Roseanne's diner, and Roseanne in turn worked with them on *GH*. Despite hopes to do likewise on *OLTL,* Roseanne never made it to Llanview.

1995

Ten years after the return of Niki Smith, a whole cast of never before seen alternate personalities suddenly emerged from inside Viki's troubled psyche. Head writers Michael Malone and Josh Griffith finally explored the real origin of Viki's disassociative identity disorder, the origin Erika Slezak herself had been hoping that some writer would acknowledge:[10] Viki had been sexually abused by her father, Victor Lord. The story line ended with the revelation that Tori, one of Viki's more homicidal alters, had murdered Victor in his hospital bed (a plot twist that Victor's return from the dead would alter down the road). From the heartbreaking realization that she had been sexually abused by her own father and had subsequently killed the man, to the demands of sliding from one vastly different personality into another, this story line gave Erika Slezak the greatest showcase any soap opera actress had ever been given to show off her range.

1996

Claire Labine and her son Matthew, who had reinvigorated *General Hospital* in the early nineties, replaced Michael Malone and Josh Griffith as head writers. Although the Labines had been applauded and won Emmys for their socially relevant story lines on *GH* (AIDS, breast cancer, organ transplants), they were not interested in continuing in that vein at *One Life to Live*.[11] They simply wanted to concentrate on character development and storytelling. Because Claire Labine had created the critically received *Ryan's Hope*, chronicling the lives of Irish immigrants in America, viewers and fans were hoping for a really exciting story line for new favorite Patrick Thornhart (Thorsten Kaye), the Irish poet turned adventure hero. They were none too happy about the twist that revealed him to have been a terrorist in his past.

Shortly after Patrick Thornhart read a poem by William Butler Yeats to his love Marty Saybrooke, the Barnes & Noble bookstore in Manhattan sold out its stock of poetry books by Yeats. When ABC discovered this fact, the network saw potential for a publishing tie-in with the show. (Previously, *Robin's Diary*, featuring the inner thoughts of *General Hospital*'s lead teen character Robin Scorpio [Kimberly McCullough] had been a best seller.) *Patrick's Notebook*, published by Hyperion and modeled after the notebook Patrick Thornhart carried around, was a combination of book and audio, intertwining poetry and personal thoughts written from the character's perspective. Thorsten Kaye not only recorded the audiotape in Patrick's brogue, he also contributed to the project a poem he himself wrote. (Ten years later, Kaye and Lloyd Bridges's widow, Dorothy, would jointly publish a collection of their own original poetry, *From Timber Ridge to Daymer Gardens*.)

1997

For the six weeks between the last episode of *The City* and the debut of *Port Charles*, ABC filled the 12:30 time slot with *A Daytime to Remember*, which rebroadcast some of the most memorable episodes of *All My Children, One Life to Live,* and *General Hospital.* Because most of the video-tapes of the early episodes had been either destroyed or taped over, the bulk of the episodes chosen came from the late seventies and onward. Soap opera fan Reba McEntire introduced the show and shared some of her own memories of watching these episodes when they first aired. Among the *One Life to Live* episodes chosen for this miniseries were Karen's courtroom admission to being a prostitute, Tina interrupting Cord's wedding to Kate Sanders (Marcia Cross), and Megan's death from lupus.

The producers made the Club Indigo set and the show itself much edgier when it hired Shequida, a gender illusionist, to play Wendi Mercury, the transgender bartender. While some viewers would have liked to see Wendy given a story line of some sort, the matter-of-fact way in which the show introduced and treated the character made a statement in and of itself. In 2001, the show would hire a man, Charles Busch, to play female modeling agency owner Peg Barlow.

1998

After *Guiding Light* fired Michael Zaslow because he was suffering from amyotrophic lateral sclerosis (ALS, also known as Lou Gehrig's Disease), he returned to *One Life,* where he had played pianist-turned-secret-agent David Renaldi from 1983 to 1986. Zaslow would have returned to *One Life* a few months earlier, but he couldn't because of his pending lawsuit against P&G.[12] Like Zaslow, David too was now battling ALS. David's wife Jenny (Brynn Thayer) had been killed in an avalanche. While there was

In the mid-1980s, pianist-turned-secret agent David Renaldi (Michael Zaslow) romanced ex-nun Jenny Jannsen (Brynn Thayer).

talk about bringing Jenny back during Zaslow's final appearances on the show, Thayer declined, not wanting Jenny's return to overshadow Zaslow's story line. Zaslow died in December that year. As one of his final requests, he asked the producers not to kill off David as well. While Zaslow could not control his own fate, he wanted David to live on, albeit off camera, as a sign of hope for everyone also battling ALS.

For the first time in its history, *One Life to Live* broadcast an episode at night. For its premiere voyage into prime time, the show promised a solution to its ongoing murder mystery, "Who Killed Georgie Phillips?" (Jennifer Bransford). Georgie, Nora Hanen's (Hillary B. Smith) assistant, had developed a fatal attraction for Nora's husband, Bo. Adding a twisted twist to the murder mystery convention of assembling the suspects together for the big reveal, Todd Manning (Roger Howarth) had taken hostage all the suspects and several family members along with them. To keep everyone in line, Todd had strapped what appeared to be a belt of dynamite around himself. The episode, which took place entirely at Viki's cabin, picked up from where that afternoon's episode had left off and ended with a shocking confession: Nora Hanen's daughter Rachel (Sandra P. Grant) had done Georgie in.

1999

As soon as *Another World* was canceled, Linda Dano, one of its premier divas, returned to *One Life to Live,* where she had played Gretel Cummings in the late 1970s. In an unprecedented move, Dano was signed to work not only on *One Life* but on all the ABC soap operas, including *General Hospital* and its spin-off *Port Charles,* which filmed on the West Coast. Dano's character, who now went by the name Rae Cummings, was supposed to better establish the connections between the soap operas, bringing fans from one show to another. Dano's daytime-spanning story line involved Rae's hunt for a child taken away from her at birth. Along the way, Rae discovered that her birth mother was *All My Children*'s Myrtle Fargate (Eileen Herlie) and that her mystery daughter was Skye Chandler (Robin Christopher), a character who herself had been transplanted to Llanview from Pine Valley. After learning that *General Hospital*'s Alan Quartermaine (Stuart Damon) was her biological father, Skye would move from Llanview to Port Charles, and Christopher would join the cast of *GH*. (The writers at *GH* would eventually undo Alan's paternity.)

2000

ABC launched SOAPnet, the first and so far only all-soap-opera cable station. SOAPnet's schedule, which includes multiple replays of that day's entire ABC lineup, gives *One Life to Live* fans a second chance to catch episodes they missed.

2001

One Life to Live became the first soap opera to incorporate animation into its story line. Producer Gary Tomlin put a spin on the daydream convention by presenting Starr Manning's (Kristen Alderson) varied fantasies as cartoons.

To honor Erika Slezak's thirtieth anniversary as Viki, New York Mayor Rudolph Giuliani declared March 16th Erika Slezak Day. Although Slezak had begun her stint on March 17, 1971, that day's title was already claimed by St. Patrick.

After planes were used as weapons in the terrorist attacks on September 11th, *One Life to Live* changed its plans for a plane crash later that fall involving Blair Cramer (Kassie DePaiva). Scenes of Blair on a plane that seemed as though it was going to crash needed to be reedited.

2002

In one of the more ambitious stunts ever attempted on daytime, *One Life to Live* went live for an entire week during the May sweeps. The last time a soap opera had broadcast live was in 1982 when the tape for an episode of *Search for Tomorrow* turned up missing. But that was only one day, and

Search was only a half-hour soap. *OLTL* executive producer Gary Tomlin promised that the live gimmick would not slow down the plotlines, which included twists like Max Holden waking up married to Roxy Balsom (Ilene Kristen). Tomlin also teased viewers with the possibility of unintentional nudity during love scenes. As a challenge for himself, he shot several scenes live from Central Park. The cast, most of whom were more than a little nervous at the idea of performing live, rose to the challenge. Kassie DePaiva (Blair Cramer) pulled off one of the week's biggest tricks, crying on cue live.

For the first time in the show's history, *One Life to Live* was presented with the Daytime Emmy for Best Drama. The award had been a long time coming. Twenty-nine years before, when it was being presented as part of the prime-time ceremony, *One Life to Live* had been one of the very first soap operas nominated for the award, known then as Outstanding Program Achievement in Daytime Drama.

2003

For years, rumors of Roger Howarth leaving the show had become almost weekly news stories for the soap press. During the ten years since he'd joined the cast, he'd already officially left twice. In 2003, he ultimately left *One Life* and joined the cast of CBS's long-running drama *As the World Turns*. Rather than introduce a new character, Howarth stepped into the role of Paul Ryan, a character who had literally grown up on the show (and a role which was being played by another actor while Howarth was negotiating with the show).

Howarth's departure forced *OLTL* to do what many had considered the impossible: recast Todd. (For many daytime fans, Todd Manning ranked up there with *General Hospital*'s Luke Spencer and *All My Children*'s Erica Kane as roles that could only be played by the person who had made them famous.) The show introduced Trevor St. John as Walker Laurence, younger brother to the villainous Mitch Laurence (Roscoe Born). As St. John caught on with the fans, the writers and producers realized that he would make a great Todd, so Walker was reinvented as Todd with plastic surgery.

2004

In an effort to unite the ABC soap operas, the writers from *All My Children* broadened a baby switch story line they were planning, to incorporate *One Life to Live*. As originally planned, *AMC*'s Bianca Montgomery (Eden Riegel) and Babe Chandler (Alexa Havins) would give birth at the same time and have their babies switched with one another's. *One Life to Live*'s Kelly Cramer (Heather Tom) then became a third party in the story line. Kelly's brother Paul (David Tom) stole Babe Chandler's newborn son and gave it to his sister, who had recently miscarried. (It had already been established that Paul was Babe's ex-husband.) The story line played out for over a year and climaxed with a three-way courtroom battle between Kelly's husband Kevin Buchanan (Dan Gauthier), Babe Chandler, and Babe's ex-husband JR Chandler (Jacob Young), who was ultimately granted custody. Along the way, Paul Cramer would be murdered, and several characters from *All My Children* considered prime suspects. The crossover also allowed for a heavyweight confrontation between two of ABC's most powerful characters and actors: Asa Buchanan (Phil Carey) and Adam Chandler (David Canary).

2005

Marcie Walsh (Kathy Brier) published her first novel, a murder mystery titled *The Killing Club*. Soon thereafter, a serial killer began reenacting murders from the novel, picking off Marcie's friends and acquaintances around Llanview. As a twist, the serial killer turned out to be two killers: Marcie's publicist Hayes Barber (Jed Orlemann) and Nick Messina (Will Bozarth), a college nemesis who had mocked her while she was writing the book. *The Killing Club* was published by Hyperion in the real world and penned by former *OLTL* head writer Michael Malone, who is also a novelist. It was, however, Marcie Walsh's name on the front cover and Kathy Brier on the talk show circuit in character—making Marcie one of the few fictional characters to ever publish a real book. (Back in the eighties, when Linda Dano was playing romance novelist Felicia Gallant on *Another World,* she published a Harlequin romance under her character's name.) *The Killing Club* became a *New York Times* Best Seller.

After Hurricane Katrina devastated New Orleans, Robin Strasser (Dorian Lord) organized her cast mates to record *One Life, Many Voices,* a CD to raise money for relief efforts. Cast members who can sing, such as Kassie DePaiva (Blair Manning), Renee Elise Goldsberry (Evangeline Williamson), and Catherine Hickland (Lindsay Rappaport), contributed a song. Kathy Brier (Marcie McBain) sang the appropriately titled "Louisiana Holiday." Robert S. Woods (Bo Buchanan) recited the lyrics to "The Star Spangled Banner." Strasser herself recited Shakespeare to background music. Beyond simply raising money, Strasser has actually rebuilt homes in New Orleans, working with Habitat for Humanity.

2006

Like her mother, Viki, Jessica Buchanan (Bree Williamson) had developed a party girl alternate personality. While Viki's alter Niki preferred dive bars, Jessica's alter, Tess, was based on socialite Paris Hilton and preferred pool parties in the Hamptons. The show promised a dark origin to Tess, concerning a topic rarely addressed on soap operas. In the spring, the audience finally learned the root of Jessica Buchanan's battle with DID: Not only had she been molested as a child by a barroom acquaintance of her mother's alter Niki Smith, the pedophile had videotaped his crime as child pornography. In one of the show's most disturbing, most heartbreaking scenes, Jessica's guilt-ridden parents Viki and Clint (now played by Jerry ver Dorn) discovered the tape and watched as much of it as they could bear.

Michael Easton (John McBain) had been involved in rather public negotiations about his contract all summer, right up to the point where John supposedly died in a fiery car crash. Fans had every reason to believe that John was actually dead. In a plot twist, D.A. Hugh Hughes (Josh Casaubon), who lay bandaged and unable to speak in a hospital bed, turned out to be John. The twist shocked eagle-eyed fans, who would have sworn that they had seen Casaubon's brown eyes peeking out from underneath the bandaging. In those first few hospital scenes, Casaubon had indeed been the one lying in the bed. When Easton agreed to stay with the show, Hugh was suddenly the one who had been buried in John's grave, while blue-eyed Easton took Casaubon's place underneath the bandages.

2007

May sweeps were scheduled to be dominated by a hostage drama at the high school. After being rejected by popular girl Britney Jennings (Portia Reiners), loner Henry (Jonathan Groff) was going to come into school with a gun, intent on killing his fellow students and then himself. Among Henry's intended targets were Britney and the show's centerpiece teen couple, Starr Manning and Cole Thornhart (Brandon Buddy). Several weeks before the story line was to begin, a student went on a killing spree on the campus of Virginia Tech college, killing thirty-two people. Although the episodes for the hostage drama had already been taped, the show ultimately decided not to broadcast them. Instead, new scenes were taped, placing the four principals (Henry, Starr, Cole, and Britney) into a car, which an overwrought and potentially suicidal Henry was driving far too quickly. Although Cole, Starr, and Britney survived, Henry was killed in the subsequent crash.

After the intensity of its May story line, *One Life to Live* lightened the mood and staged *Prom Night The Musical.* As Starr and Cole prepared to attend the prom—with other people—they would burst into song to reflect the way they were feeling. The show also took advantage of the musical talents of Starr's on-screen mom Kassie DePaiva (Blair Cramer), who sang a song about watching her little girl grow up. Kathy Brier, who had starred on Broadway in *Hairspray* and whose Marcie was now teaching at the school, was also given a solo number. For fans of Starr and Cole, the prom ended on a high note, reuniting them as a couple.

Dustin Hoffman, who was researching soap operas for the film *Last Chance Harvey,* in which he plays an aging soap opera actor, stopped by the *One Life to Live* studios for a look at what goes on behind the scenes. As it turned out, he picked a big day, when the cast was rehearsing for its *Prom Night* musical. Later Hoffman visited the *General Hospital* studio in Los Angeles, which he had previously visited in 1981, while researching soaps for the film *Tootsie*, in which he played an actor posing as a soap opera actress.

On August 17, *One Life to Live* aired its 10,000th episode. To mark the occasion, the writers killed off and buried Asa Buchanan (Phil Carey), who had been with the show since 1980. Earlier in the year, when Carey was taken off contract, he rejected the show's offer to stick around on a recurring basis. The death of Asa allowed for the return of several audience favorites from the past: Nathan Fillion (Joey Buchanan), James DePaiva (Max Holden), John Loprieno (Cord Roberts), Dan Gauthier (Kevin Buchanan), and Tonja Walker (Alex Olanov).

On again/off again couple Todd Manning (now Trevor St. John) and Blair Cramer (Kassie DePaiva) became husband and wife for a fifth time, breaking the old record held by *All My Children*'s Cliff and Nina.

What D.I.D. "They" Do?

Does Victoria Lord Riley Buchanan Carpenter Davidson have more alternate personalities than Erika Slezak has Emmy awards? That remains one of my all-time favorite soap opera trivia questions. At the moment, there's a tie: six Emmys, six alters. Once Slezak wins her seventh Emmy (which, based on her track record, she will more than likely do in the future), she can finally have one Emmy for Viki and one for each of her alters.

Viki's alternate personality Niki Smith played a significant role during *One Life to Live*'s early years. For a show that prided itself on exploring the relations between classes, Niki Smith presented the ultimate bridge: a working-class fragment of the terribly upper-crust Victoria Lord. The split personality also created a unique love triangle for soap operas at the time: Viki loved fellow reporter Joe Riley (Lee Patterson) while Niki had a thing for mechanic Vinnie Wolek (then Anthony Ponzini).

Once "cured" by psychiatrist Dr. Polk (then Donald

Moffat), Niki stayed put for a solid fifteen years. Niki Smith was referred to from time to time, but she did not re-emerge until the mid-1980s. Since then, her reappearances have become increasingly frequent. She now tends to pop up every couple of years—usually when Viki's life has been running a tad too smoothly.

In keeping with new information on Dissociative Identity Disorder (D.I.D.)—namely, the discovery that patients rarely exhibit only one alternate personality—Niki eventually turned out to be one of many lurking inside Viki:

1. Niki Smith
   The most frequent personality to take control, Niki seemed the complete opposite to Viki. Whereas Viki was proper (some, including Niki, would say uptight), Viki was completely uninhibited, with the brassy red wig and leopard-print wardrobe to prove it. During her first emergences, Niki came across more as a party girl than a villainess; in recent years, namely since being integrated with Viki's other alters, Niki has displayed a more dangerous side, shooting innocent people and pushing Viki's husband out the window.

2. Tommy
   One of the only two male personalities inside Viki, Tommy embodied all her rage at having been victimized in her youth. Tommy also symbolizes the son her father always wanted, the son who probably would not have been victimized. Tommy first emerged on-screen during an argument between Viki and Dorian, in which Dorian admitted that she knew all about Victor Lord sexually

abusing Viki. Short on words and quick with his fists, Tommy knocked Dorian down a flight of stairs.

3. Jean Randolph
   Named after Viki's mother, Eugenia Randolph Lord, Jean Randolph considers herself the gatekeeper in Viki's mind. She sees it as her mission to protect Viki from any and all painful truths. While not intrinsically evil, Jean Randolph will do whatever is necessary to keep Viki safe. If that requires imprisoning Dorian Lord in the basement of Llanfair, so be it. The most well-spoken and well-mannered of Viki's alters, Jean Randolph comes across the most Viki-like, with one noticeable omission: She embodies none of Viki's warmth, not even toward Viki's children. While Niki Smith tends to favor red wigs, Jean Randolph's prop of choice is a pair of eyeglasses.

4. Princess
   The most pitiable of Viki's alters, Princess is Viki from an almost infantile stage, the stage before her innocence was violated and lost forever.

5. Tori
   If Niki is the antithesis to Viki, then Tori (a shortened form of Victoria's own name) is the antithesis to Jean Randolph. While Jean Randolph has devoted her life to keeping secrets, Tori wants to see the truth, the whole truth, come out. Of all Viki's personalities, including Tommy in full rage, Tori is the most dangerous. She killed—or thought she killed—Viki's father, Victor

Lord, in his hospital bed. She also set fire to the offices of *The Banner*, Llanfair, and even Victor's mausoleum.

6. Victor Lord
   It is not uncommon for abuse victims to harbor the personality of their abusers. In one of the creepiest moments in *One Life to Live*'s history, the Victor Lord personality emerged during a conversation between Viki and Jessica, whom he reached out to touch before Viki regained control.

Since Viki was first treated by Dr. Polk in the 1960s, several explanations have been offered for why Viki's personality fractured:

1. As a little girl, Viki thought that she had witnessed her father killing her mother. While Viki had seen her mother's death, the circumstances surrounding it had been misinterpreted. Yes, her mother and father had been arguing at the top of the stairs at Llanfair, but her father had not pushed his wife down the stairs. She had slipped during the argument and fallen. Viki's coming to that revelation in the late 1960s seemed to cure her of her need for the Niki personality.

2. As a college student, Viki had walked in on her father having sex with her roommate and best friend, Irene Manning. Viki became completely unhinged by this experience and her father's choice of sex partner, a woman young enough to be his own daughter. This

revelation laid the foundation for the ultimate explanation, which was still ten years away. The memories of her father's indiscretion remained buried inside Viki until Tina Clayton (Andrea Evans) returned to town in the mid-1980s and unearthed proof that she was Victor Lord's daughter.

3. While a teenager, Viki had fallen in love with Roger Gordon (Larry Pine), a teenage boy who lived in an underground city built by Viki's father. The fact that Victor Lord had built an underground city was a lot for a child, even an intelligent child like Victoria Lord, to comprehend. Unfortunately, seeing her first love blown up and presumably killed as he was reentering that city proved to be the trauma that Viki could not handle. At that moment, Niki Smith emerged to carry the grief. This explanation was offered in the late 1980s after Viki discovered that nearly an entire year of her life had been forgotten, a year that included her giving birth to a child.

4. In the early 1990s, the show finally decided to address the real reason why Niki had been created, the dirty truth that had lain hidden for so many years: Viki had been sexually abused by her own father. Niki, a character of nearly pure id, could take control and enjoy the sex as a physical pleasure while a horrified and humiliated Viki hid inside her own mind.

Although Viki's alternate personalities were presumably integrated in the mid-1990s, Niki Smith has managed to sneak out from time to time. The secret that Mitch Laurence,

the psychopath who had murdered Niki's lover Harry
O'Neill, had not only raped Viki but was her daughter
Jessica's biological father gave Niki the leverage she needed
to take control again. She was aided by Viki's friend Rae
Cummings, who wasn't as well qualified to be performing
hypnotherapy as she pretended. Rae didn't realize that Niki
was still in control when she walked out of the office.

Years later, when Viki's own daughter Jessica developed D.I.D., Viki was forced to bring Niki out to learn the
source of Jessica's problems: Niki wasn't trolling the dive
bars on her own all those years ago; no, she was dragging
little Jessica along with her. One of the men in the bar not
only molested Jessica, he taped it as child pornography.

As Jessica's battle with D.I.D. illustrates, mental illness
tends to run in families. If you need further proof, just look
at the Cramers. Dorian's mother lived in a fantasy world
where she did nothing but play piano all day. Both of
Dorian's sisters, Addie and Melinda, have been institution-
alized over the years. Dorian's daughter Cassie suffered a
complete mental breakdown after her miscarriage. Even Blair,
presumably the strongest member of the next generation,
tried to kill herself after a failed love affair and shot one of
her husbands in a blind rage. Viki Buchanan is not worry-
ing over nothing when it comes to the mental health of her
family members:

- Megan Gordon
  Because of her own battles with Niki Smith, Viki had
  worried about her oldest daughter, Megan, an actress
  playing a split personality on her soap opera. The
  character of Ruby Bright, with tight, flashy clothes

and gaudy jewelry, resembled Niki Smith just a little too closely for Viki's comfort. When Megan witnessed Viki getting shot, she (Megan) immediately retreated into her soap opera character for weeks. Aside from this one incident, Ruby did not take over again before Megan's untimely demise.

- Todd Manning
After holding his family and the Buchanans hostage at his cabin, Todd seemed to develop D.I.D. Different personalities emerged, such as Tom and Rod (as though he'd split his own name in half). From sister Viki, he'd obviously learned that you can't just have one alter and be believed. Just as Viki had Tommy and her father, Todd developed a female alter named Miss Perkins, a prissy sort of woman who out-Vikied Viki. While Todd had not been sexually molested by his adoptive father, he had been physically abused by the man his whole life. Todd, it turned out, was faking his D.I.D. to avoid a jail sentence. When his daughter, Starr, who could see through his charade, began faking an alter of her own named Suzie, Todd called an end to his scam. Viki was devastated that Todd would exploit her illness for his own benefit.

- Jessica Buchanan
Like mother, like daughter. Jessica not only developed a split personality, she gave her a name that rhymed (close enough) with her own: Tess. Although Tess frequented swankier sorts of establishments—pool parties in the Hamptons rather than dives along the waterfront—Tess

was still just as much a party girl as Niki. Because of Niki Smith's complicity in Jess's D.I.D., Niki could be considered Tess's mother. For the moment, Tess seems to be integrated with Jessica, but as her mother's history has shown, integration doesn't always stick.

2
Casting Call

I Wanna Be a Soap Star

Sometimes, winning isn't everything. During the 2006 season of SOAPnet's reality competition *I Wanna Be a Soap Star,* ten actors and actresses vied for a contract role on *One Life to Live.* Although Mikey Jerome won, his character was killed off at the end of that thirteen-week contract. Third-place finisher BethAnn Bonner, on the other hand, caught the attention of *OLTL* casting director Julie Madison, who was judging the competition, and wound up with a contract of her own as police officer Talia Sahid.

While casting roles is almost never televised like this, the process often involves an equal amount of drama and those last minute-surprises . . .

When it came to the character of Carla Benari, a young black woman passing herself off as white, Agnes Nixon made clear to the casting director the fact that she wanted a light-skinned black actress for the role. She did not want a white actress as had been done in feature films that had dealt with the same topic. Much to Nixon's dismay, agents kept sending over white actresses. She had nearly abandoned hope of finding the right actress for what she thought would be one of the show's landmark story lines when she came across an article in *The New York Times* written by Ellen Holly. In the piece, Holly detailed the difficulties and prejudices she faced as a light-skinned black actress. Carla's story line, it should be noted, was inspired by singer/actress Eartha Kitt, whom Nixon had watched on a talk show, discussing her own problems of being a light-skinned black woman. By the time Nixon finished Holly's article, she knew that she had just found her Carla.

Clint Ritchie nearly turned down the role of Clint Buchanan. He wasn't too keen on moving to New York and leaving his horses back in California.[13]

Worried about the impending actors strike in 1980, Ritchie's on-screen pa Phil Carey (Asa Buchanan), who had worked primarily in feature films and prime time, had told his agent to specifically look for something on daytime. (Soap opera actors belonged to the union AFTRA, which was separate from the Screen Actors Guild.)

Fiona Hutchison (Gabrielle Medina), who had spent the early part of her life in Jamaica, had been advised to drop her accent in order to widen her acting opportunities. *OLTL* executive producer Paul Rauch, who hired her, told Hutchison that he was glad that she didn't take that advice, because he had hired her in part *because of* her accent.

Jessica Tuck (Megan Gordon) had been working at the same catering service as Bronwen Booth, who originated the role of Andy Harrison (Megan's future sister-in-law). The night before Tuck was to begin playing Megan, she burned her uniform.

Susan Batten so charmed casting director Ellen Novack

that she was hired to create the character of Luna Moody without any specific story line in mind.

Tuc Watkins was the seventh actor called in to audition opposite Robin Strasser (Dorian Lord) for the role of David Vickers. The scene called for David to surprise Dorian with a kiss. Watkins surmised that Strasser had gone beyond the point where any actor's kiss was going to surprise her. Instead, he caught Strasser and the casting director off guard by refusing to kiss her and laughing at her instead.

During his first audition to play RJ Gannon, then being called Jimmy Glover, Timothy Stickney accidentally knocked over a lamp. When the producers asked him if he'd like to try the scene again rather than simply telling him to leave, Stickney suspected that they might actually want him for the role.

When the role of Dr. Paige Miller was originally being introduced as a love interest for Bo Buchanan, the producers offered it to Mary Beth Evans, who came very, *very* close to accepting. (Back when Evans was first playing nurse Kayla Brady on *Days of Our Lives,* Robert S. Woods picked her as the actress on another soap opera opposite whom he most wanted to work.) Although Evans liked the role of Paige, *As the World Turns,* where she had been recurring, suddenly offered her a contract to keep her from leaving, a contract she accepted. *One Life to Live* hired *The Young and the Restless/The Bold and the Beautiful* alumna Kimberlin Brown.

Some actors simply get their lucky break early on. The role of Marcie McBain (then known as Marcie Walsh and only slated to last for two episodes), was the very first television or movie role for which Kathy Brier ever auditioned.

While most students graduate from college unsure where

they will end up working, Melissa Gallo was spared that worry. She was offered the role of Adriana Cramer the same day she finished taking her last final exam at NYU.

Melissa Archer slept right through her alarm clock the day that she was scheduled to audition for the role of Natalie Buchanan. As luck would have it, hers was one of the very last names to be called, so no one at ABC realized that she had shown up late.

When John-Paul Lavoisier read for the role of Rex Balsom, he channeled *OLTL* alum Ryan Phillippe's performance as a scheming womanizer in the film *Cruel Intentions*.

Forbes March had just unpacked the last box at his new home in Los Angeles when *One Life to Live* came looking for him to play the role of Nash Brennan. Not wanting to move back east, he initially turned down the offer.

When *Port Charles* was reaching the end of its run in 2003, Michael Easton had become a highly desired actor because of his performance as a vampire rock star. *One Life to Live* offered him the chance to take over the role of Todd Manning, one of the more dynamic characters on daytime. Easton turned down the opportunity, not wanting to step into a role so closely affiliated with another actor. Instead, he took the show up on its counteroffer to create a brand-new character he could make all his own, John McBain.

When John Brotherton was going into the audition to play Jared Banks, his agent told him to envision the character of con artist Sawyer on the ABC series *Lost*. Since Brotherton didn't watch the show, he needed to brush up on the character by watching old episodes.

Big Shoes to Fill

E rika Slezak is a recast. So is Robin Strasser. Even Todd Manning, a role once considered to be Roger Howarth's sole property, has not only been recast, but recast quite successfully. While replacing a popular actor is a casting director's nightmare, it has been done time and time again.

When the role of Anna Craig was being recast in 1978, Phyllis Behar was more than a little familiar with the character. She and her husband, Hank, had been writers on the show for the previous three years. Behar not only knew Anna, she loved the character and believed that she was the best person to play her.[14]

Susan Keith literally cried when she was offered the role of Samantha Vernon—and they were not tears of joy. Keith had originally been auditioning to play Faith Kipling when Julie Montgomery left the show mid–story line. Desperate for a replacement, the producers offered the role to Keith, who knew that they really didn't want her. And she was right. The entire time Keith was on, the producers were trying to lure Montgomery back. As soon as they did, Keith was let go. She did land on her feet, however, getting the part of Cecile dePoulignac on *Another World*.[15]

Few actresses have left their imprint on a character the way Andrea Evans did with Tina Lord. When Evans left in 1990, *One Life to Live* launched an incredible casting call to find the next Tina. (The show had recast the character unsuccessfully in the mid-eighties, before Evans returned.) More than three hundred actresses read for the part before it was given to Karen Witter, a virtual unknown. The casting directors suspected that she could win over the audience, at least the male portion of it, when a number of the show's actors went out of their way to strike up a conversation with Witter during the audition.

When the wildly popular James DePaiva opted to leave the show in 1990, the producers employed the old plastic surgery convention. Max Holden was presumed to have died in a fiery car crash but had survived, just terribly burned. A plastic surgeon gave him a new face, that of Nicholas Walker, who had played Trey Clegg on the CBS soap opera *Capitol*. When DePaiva agreed to come back, *One Life* jumped at the chance to get the original back. As for the fact that Max supposedly looked different enough now for his own lover Gabrielle (Fiona Hutchison) not to recognize him, that issue was never addressed. On his first day back, DePaiva looked into the camera and said, "I feel like the old Max." For the audience at home, happy to have their old favorite back, that served as acknowledgment enough.

When Jensen Buchanan's run as Sarah Gordon was winding down, the producers were trying to find her replacement. They hoped to lure daytime superstar Genie Francis

(Laura Spencer, *General Hospital*) to the show, but she ultimately chose to head to *All My Children,* where Agnes Nixon was creating a role just for her.

Although Cady Huffman was a Tony Award winner (2001 Best Featured Actress in a Musical for *The Producers*), she didn't think that she stood a good chance of landing the role of Dr. Paige Miller, which was being vacated by Kimberlin Brown. So pessimistic was Huffman that she blew off the audition to go to the beach. She was shocked when the casting directors called her a few days later to let her know that they were still interested.

David Tom took over the role of Paul Cramer, playing on-screen brother to his real-life sister Heather Tom, who had recently taken over the role of Kelly Cramer. The two had nearly worked as brother and sister on *The Young and the Restless,* where Heather played Victoria Newman for more than a decade. David auditioned to play Victoria's younger brother Nicholas. While he didn't get that role, he wound up playing Billy Abbott, a role unrelated to Victoria. As such, they never worked in any story lines together. (The Toms are not the only brother and sister who have worked together on *OLTL.* Although Matthew Buchanan and Starr Manning are not related to each other, they are played by brother and sister Eddie Alderson and Kristen Alderson.)

Just two days after learning that he was being reduced to recurring at *Guiding Light,* where he'd been working steadily since 1979, Jerry ver Dorn was sitting in the *One Life to Live* office discussing the possibility of taking over the role of Clint Buchanan. Mark Derwin (Clint's half-brother Ben Davidson), who had worked with ver

Dorn at *Guiding Light,* recommended him for the role. While discussing the possibility of joining *One Life,* the usually cleanshaven ver Dorn grew a mustache to affect a more rugged physical appearance. The mustache, however, was gone by his first day on the set.

Whenever Bree Williamson auditioned for roles on *One Life to Live,* she always heard that she looked too much like Erin Torpey, who played Jessica Buchanan.[16] It was more than fitting then that Williamson should land the role of Jessica when Torpey opted to leave the show. Her first day on the set, Williamson received a bouquet of flowers from Torpey, who told her that she could call anytime with questions about the show and/or the character of Jessica.

When Nathan Fillion was recast into the role of Joey Buchanan, Kirk Geiger, himself a recast, playing the ninth Kevin Buchanan, realized that his own days on the show were numbered. Half a foot shorter than Fillion, Geiger sensed that Kevin was not coming across on-screen as Joey's older brother. While the producers told Geiger that he was being let go in favor of an actor that looked older, Geiger told *Soap Opera Digest* what he suspected: They were looking for someone taller.

The role of Viki's older son Kevin Buchanan had been recast so often that Dan Gauthier was nicknamed Kevin Eleven when he became the eleventh actor to play the part.

Up until Kevin Buchanan, Dan Wolek was the role famous for being constantly recast. As longtime character Larry Wolek's only son and Viki's nephew, Dan Wolek should have been a central character. After the sixth try, the show finally gave up on Dan in the early nineties. During the early eighties, the character was literally being recast once a year, prompting one producer to deem it "the role from hell."[17]

Two Roles to Play

One of the reasons so many cast members enjoyed the Wild West story line was that it gave them a second role into which they could sink their teeth. Even Erika Slezak, who had just completed a much heralded turn as Viki's alter Niki Smith, loved creating schoolmarm Miss Ginny. Brenda Brock so impressed the producers with her turn as May McGillis during that Wild West saga that they signed her on to play May's lookalike descendant Brenda McGillis (whom they named after her). Throughout its history, *One Life to Live* has offered many of its actors the chance to try their hand with a second role.

When Gerald Anthony created pimp Marco Dane's good twin Dr. Mario Correlli, he not only shaved off Marco's beard, Anthony consciously changed the character's walk and the pitch of his speaking voice.

When talk show host Pat Ashley's (Jacqueline Courtney) brunette but otherwise lookalike sister Maggie (also played by Courtney) showed up at her doorstep, viewers

In the Old West, Clint Buchanan (then Clint Ritchie) courted his wife Viki's lookalike ancestor, Miss Ginny (Erika Slezak).

realized that it was only a matter of time before Maggie bleached her hair and stole her sister's life. For Courtney, who had been cast as the tragic heroine throughout her soap career, Maggie offered her the chance to finally play the bad girl.

When Robert S. Woods returned to the show in 1988, viewers initially found something off about his portrayal. He no longer felt like the Bo Buchanan they had missed—and with good reason. This Bo turned out to be Patrick London, who had undergone plastic surgery as part of an elaborate scheme to get his hands on the Buchanan fortune. Ironically, Woods told *Soap Opera Digest,* Faux Bo felt closer to the original concept of Bo than what he had been playing his last few years on the show.

The character of Joe Riley had been dead seven years when Lee Patterson received a phone call asking him if he would be interested in coming back as Joe's never-before-mentioned twin Tom Dennison. At first, Patterson nearly hung up, thinking that someone was playing a joke on him.[18] During his return, Patterson did revive Joe briefly when Viki took her famous trip up to Heaven.

Although Carlo Hesser (Thom Christopher) offered moments of dark humor, especially when paired opposite Tonja Walker as Alex Olanov, the far more timid character of Egyptologist Mortimer Bern gave Christopher an opportunity to really show off his comic skills.

Although Dr. Colin MacIver was slated to die in a murder mystery, the show recognized the immense popularity of Ty Treadway, who played him. At the reading of Colin Mac-Iver's will, Treadway showed up as twin brother Troy, who was also a doctor and would also develop an infatuation with Nora Hanen. By the end of Treadway's run, Troy turned out to be just as crazy as his brother.

As if stepping into the role of Todd Manning wasn't a big enough feat for his first year on the job, Trevor St. John also took on the daunting task of a second role. Not only was St. John playing Todd, who had undergone plastic surgery to look like Walker Laurence, he also played Walker himself. Although Walker was a ruthless mobster, St. John consciously chose to play the role completely against type as quiet and somewhat soft.

As Todd's eccentric lawyer/right-hand woman Mrs. Bigelow, Patricia O'Connell added a comic dimension to the show. Fans felt the loss when Mrs. Bigelow was killed off by Todd's kidnapper Margaret Cochran (Tari Signor), but O'Connell returned briefly as the ironically named Hazel Smalls. Hazel lived down the way from the cabin where Todd was being held captive. While both Blair and Todd noted Hazel's similarity to Mrs. Bigelow, O'Connell's second turn on the show was criminally short-lived.

No actor has ever been brought back to a show quite like Nathaniel Marston. Al Holden's death completely ticked off the fans, who loved his romance with Marcie Walsh. Rather than undo Al's death or bring him back as a looka-like, the writers borrowed a story line from the film *Heaven Can Wait,* which itself was a remake of *Here Comes Mr. Jordan.* Al's soul returned to Earth in the body of the obnoxious Dr. Michael McBain (a role originated by R. Brandon Johnson), who died of an allergic reaction to his medication. As soon as Michael's soul left the body, Al's jumped in just in time for Marcie to bring the body back to life via CPR. As soon as Al took control of Michael's body, Nathaniel Marston took over the role. (No mention was made of Michael suddenly looking like Al Holden.) As Michael, Al set about winning over his grieving girlfriend Marcie without letting on who he really was. Once Marcie fell in love with "Michael," the Al persona disappeared, but Marston stayed around as though he'd been playing Michael from the start.

Two Roles to Play—Take Two

Kale Browne (Sam Rappaport), who had been living with Catherine Hickland (Lindsay Rappaport) and her then husband Michael E. Knight (Tad Martin, *All My Children*), recommended Hickland for the role of Sam's ex-wife. Hickland didn't learn of Browne's involvement until long after she took the role. Which she almost didn't do. Since the gig was only slated for one day, she was afraid that taking it would lock her out of consideration for longer-term roles on the show.[19] A legitimate concern, but not an absolute. A number of actors have appeared on the show in small roles, even as extras, before coming back. Chris Stack had a small role as a drug dealer before taking over the role of Dr. Michael McBain. David Fumero had played a police detective one year before taking over the role of Cristian Vega. Like Fumero, Kale Browne had been one of Llanview's finest years before he was cast as lawyer Sam Rappaport. While casting directors do shy away from hiring alumni to play different roles, sometimes the right actor for a given role is a familiar face.

Larry Pine, who played Viki's ancestor Randolph Lord during the Wild West story, returned later that same year to play Roger Gordon, the father of Viki's secret child—not that viewers were supposed to speculate on the resemblance between Viki's one-time lover and her great-great-grandfather.

When it comes to styling hair, Llanview's queen of the malapropism, Roxy Balsom, isn't half bad. Then again, it's not rocket science. Yet when actress Ilene Kristen first appeared in 1982, her character, Georgina Whitman, was exactly that, a rocket scientist.

Crime family heir Alex Crown, played by Roy Thinnes in the mid-eighties, had supposedly been killed off, the victim of a contract slaying, only to return from the dead a

Before General Sloan Carpenter (Roy Thinnes, right) wooed Viki Lord Buchanan (Erika Slezak, middle) away from husband Clint Buchanan (then Clint Ritchie, left), Thinnes had played crime family heir Alex Crown.

few months later—courtesy of a bulletproof vest. Thinnes returned to the show a few years later, this time as General Sloan Carpenter, who would become Viki's fourth husband. Sloan's death, from cancer, has proven a bit more permanent than Alex Crown's.

Matthew Ashford's Dr. Drew Ralston left Llanview in a body bag in 1983, the victim of a robbery gone bad. Twenty years later, the actor returned, once again playing a doctor, Dr. Stephen Haver. Instead of getting killed this time, Ashford's character was the one committing murder, numerous murders, as the infamous Music Box Killer.

In 1978, shortly before joining the cast of *The Doctors,* Kim Zimmer held Llanview Hospital hostage as Bonnie Harmer, an escaped fugitive. After *The Doctors* was canceled, Zimmer returned to *One Life* as a character aptly named Echo. This time, while making life hell for newlyweds Viki and Clint Buchanan, she was the one taken hostage by an escaped convict.

In 1997, during a location shoot in New York City, Randolph Mantooth crossed his character Alex Masters over from *The City,* which was set in New York. A private investigator, Alex assisted Commissioner Bo Buchanan with a manhunt. Mantooth's second stint on the show, as suspected arsonist Kirk Harmon, placed him at odds with Bo.

Mantooth's *Loving* wife Lisa Peluso has been brought onto *One Life* twice, both times as a vixen to complicate the romance of a popular couple. As bad girl Billie Giordano in the late eighties, Peluso tried to lure Wade Coleman (Doug Wert) away from ultrasweet Mari Lynn Dennison. In 2001, she returned as really bad girl (as in mob-connected)

Gina Russo, who kidnapped Viki to keep her away from Ben Davidson.

During his Kevin Buchanan audition, Kevin Stapleton never mentioned that he had already appeared on *One Life to Live* back in the late eighties. He had played one of the actors working with Kevin's half-sister Megan Gordon on the soap-within-a-soap *Fraternity Row*. He didn't want any of the casting directors wondering why the show hadn't kept him around.

When it comes to playing different roles, Christine Jones holds a unique distinction: She is the only actor to have been given contracts for three different characters over the years. In 1975, she was Nurse Sheila Rafferty. Five years later, when Erika Slezak took her maternity leave, Jones filled in as Viki. Five years after that, Jones returned as Pamela Stuart, Asa Buchanan's secret wife.

The Guests Are Arriving

The judge presiding in the custody battle over Ace Buchanan that spanned both *One Life to Live* and *All My Children* was played by one of TV's favorite mothers, Michael Learned from *The Waltons*. In what has become a tradition for the show, when possible, celebrities are hired to sit in the judge's seat during the bigger trials. When Tina Lord was accused of murdering Harry O'Neill, Frances Sternhagen, best known as Cliff Clavin's mother on *Cheers* and Charlotte's mother-in-law, Bunny, on *Sex and the City*, presided over the trial. As Judge "Killer" Carlin, stage and screen actor Tony Roberts sent Gabrielle Medina to prison. After the cancellation of *Search for Tomorrow*, soap legend Mary Stuart came to *One Life to Live* for a short stint as a corrupt judge in the trial where Mari Lynn Dennison was indicted for shooting her mother to death. Other celebrity judges have included Ruby Dee, Milo O'Shea, Philip Bosco, and Frank Cover from *The Jeffersons*. They are but a handful of celebrities who have popped up in Llanview over the years.

Four-time Best Actress Oscar nominee Marsha Mason (*The Goodbye Girl*) had been spending time on the *One Life to Live* set, observing the directors with her eye toward making the transition from acting into directing. Supervising producer Robyn Goodman and executive producer Linda Gottlieb, who were friends of Mason, allowed her to direct the occasional scene. Mason was planning on being on the set the day the show taped Max Holden and Luna Moody's wedding. When Gottlieb asked if she would like to step in front of the camera and play the priestess presiding over the ceremony, Mason agreed.

Regis Philbin had already played himself on *All My Children* and recurred as a politician on *Ryan's Hope* when he guested on *One Life to Live* alongside his *Live with Regis and Kelly* cohost Kelly Ripa, herself a former soap actress (Hayley Vaughan, *All My Children*). Appropriately enough for talk show hosts, all *One Life to Live* wanted was their voices. Philbin and Ripa lent their vocals to one of Starr Manning's animated fantasies, in which she imagined herself a guest on their show.

Much of the action during the show's 6,000th episode took place in Atlantic City. Ivana Trump guested on the show as herself, the owner of a casino named Ivana's, an obvious spoof on her ex-husband Donald's eponymously named Atlantic City hotel and casino.

Alex Olanov enlisted the aid of sex therapist Dr. Ruth to transform meek Mortimer Bern (Thom Christopher) into the sexually dynamic Carlo Hesser. Years later, Dr. Ruth would become the inspiration for the character of sex therapist Dr. Maud (Helen Gallagher).

Mortimer Bern's mother was played by both an Academy

Award and three-time Emmy winner, Eileen Heckart (*But-terflies Are Free*), and a Tony Award winner and Broadway legend, Elaine Stritch.

For the story-line shocker that Dorian Lord's mother Sonya was still alive, the show hired Tony Award winner Marian Seldes (*A Delicate Balance*) to play the Cramer family's unbalanced matriarch.

Ilene Kristen (Roxy Balsom) got no less than Oscar nominee Sylvia Miles from *Midnight Cowboy* to play Roxy's mother, Stella.

Kojak and *Knots Landing* alumnus Kevin Dobson was chosen for a high-profile stint on *OLTL,* as Pennsylvania Governor Harrison Brooks.

To give its Daytime Emmy spoof the Daisy Awards a touch of realism, the show hired *Lifestyles of the Rich and Famous* host Robin Leach to emcee the event while one-hit-wonder Information Society ("What's On Your Mind") performed.

Tony Award–nominated writer Charles Busch (*The Tale of the Allergist's Wife*) is most recognizable to audiences for his recurring role as a cross-dressing inmate on the HBO prison drama *Oz,* as well as for playing a Lana Turner–style leading lady in the independent film *Die, Mommie, Die!* He was surprised when *One Life to Live* wanted him to play modeling agency owner Peg Barlow. He agreed to the guest spot as long as it did not end with someone pulling off Peg's wig to reveal that she was really a man.[20]

Frank McCourt, author of the international best-selling memoir *Angela's Ashes,* detailing his poverty-stricken life in Ireland, agreed to a book signing in Llanview as a favor to his brother Malachy McCourt, who was playing Irish terrorist Thomas Kenneally. The two taped a scene together in which Frank asked Malachy if he did any writing himself, to which Malachy replied, "My brother is the writer in the family."

First, You Cry, Betty Rollin's memoir about her battle with breast cancer, was celebrating its twenty-fifth anniversary the same year that Viki (Erika Slezak) was fighting her own battle with breast cancer. Since Rollin was a former editor at such magazines as *Vogue* and was also a news correspondent for NBC, it made sense that she would know newspaper editor and owner Viki Lord Davidson. Rollin popped up on the show to offer Viki support and promote the reissue of her own memoir.

In the mid-to-late seventies, *One Life to Live* and *General Hospital*'s schedules were flipped around to better survive against the powerhouse game show *Match Game.* By 1982, with *Match Game* at the end of its run, host Gene Rayburn popped up on *OLTL* as Quentin Frazier, a congressman in Asa's pocket.

Although *Man from U.N.C.L.E.* Robert Vaughn had left *As the World Turns* unhappy with the soap opera experience, he did agree to a short stint on *One Life to Live* as a bishop.

A pre–*Arrested Development* Jessica Walter showed up on *One Life to Live* as Eleanor Armitage, the mistress to another bishop.

Magician Penn Jillette, half of the team Penn & Teller, gave Tina Lord (Karen Witter) a makeover as hairstylist Rudy.

Joy Behar and Elisabeth Hasselbeck played themselves when baseball player turned underwear model (and secret white supremacist/arsonist) Tate Harmon (Chris Beetem) came on *The View* and hopped all over the furniture, proclaiming his love for Adriana Cramer—a scene inspired by Tom Cruise's couch-jumping declaration of love for Katie Holmes on *Oprah*.

One Life to Live gave Bo Buchanan and Nora Hanen the ultimate rock-and-roll wedding, complete with the legendary Little Richard. He not only presided over the ceremony, he also performed a few of his songs, some of which he forgot the lyrics to. While soap opera weddings are notorious for taping late into the night, Little Richard could not stick around; he was performing at 7:00 that night. The producers, who had been taking their time, did not know about Little Richard's previous engagement until 6:00. Production sped up to get him out of the studio in time.

While singer Erykah Badu was not a fan of the show, her grandmother had been watching it for years. Badu agreed to perform under the condition that her grandmother be allowed on set during the taping. Badu's grandmother was not only allowed on the set, she was seated in the scene with Kassie DePaiva's Blair, whom she loved, along with her favorite new couple, Mel and Dorian (Stephen Markle and Robin Strasser).

Nelly Furtado, who had scored a number one smash with "Promiscuous Girl" during the summer of 2006, didn't want to simply come out and sing a song when she performed on *One Life to Live* during the February sweeps. She wanted the chance to act a little as well.[21] The writers created a backstory for her and Antonio Vega (Kamar de los Reyes), in whose club she would be appearing. The two, it turned out, had known each other when they were growing up. When Nelly Furtado was working on the show, Brandon Buddy (Cole Thornhart) really wanted to go over and introduce himself to her, but he was intimidated by her bodyguards.[22]

When Tito Puente, Jr., a personal friend of Ilene Kristen (Roxy Balsom), performed at Capricorn in early 2006, Kamar de los Reyes (Antonio Vega), who plays drums, got the opportunity to play alongside him.

Country star Bill Anderson made several visits to the show in the late seventies/early eighties, tied in with Becky Lee Abbott (Mary Gordon Murray) and Johnny Drummond's (Wayne Massey) rising music careers. When the show traveled to Nashville for Becky Lee and Johnny's debut at the Grand Ole Opry, Anderson introduced them.

During the romance of Marty Saybrooke and Irish poet/adventurer Patrick Thornhart, the couple was serenaded by The Chieftains, a group appropriately enough from Ireland. The Chieftains performed "Song Without End," which figured heavily into Marty and Patrick's story line—the music contained a hidden code they were trying to decipher. Fans were more interested in where they could get a copy of the song, which had become an audience favorite.

Through the years, the nightspots around Llanview have hosted musical acts ranging from Peter Allen to Kool & the Gang, from The Beach Boys to rapper Timbaland. Even opera has come to the soap opera, as famed diva Roberta Peters sang at Clint and Viki's 1982 wedding.

Roles That Got Away

Try to imagine a soap opera starring both Susan Lucci and Erika Slezak. That would have been the case had Slezak been hired for the first soap for which she auditioned. She read for the role of nurse Mary Kennicott on *All My Children*.

Now try to imagine anybody but Susan Lucci as *All My Children*'s Erica Kane. When the show was being launched, the casting directors saw hundreds of young actresses, among them Patricia Mauceri (Carlotta Vega).

While *All My Children* did not consider Phil Carey (Asa Buchanan) right for the role of Palmer Cortlandt, which went to the more refined James Mitchell, a former ballet dancer, Carey's audition tape did bring him to the attention of the *One Life to Live* casting director.

When the role of *Days of Our Lives* hero Roman Brady was first being cast, Kale Browne (Sam Rappaport) read for the part.

Robin Strasser (Dorian Lord) was on the short list of actresses being considered to take over the much coveted role

Asa Buchanan (Phil Carey) with three-time wife Renée Divine (Patricia Elliott).

of *Guiding Light*'s Alexandra Spaulding, which had been originated by soap legend Beverlee McKinsey. Before joining another soap opera, Strasser checked to see if *One Life* was interested in having her back, and it was.

When Genie Francis (Laura Spencer) announced that she was leaving *General Hospital*, the show searched for an actress to play a Laura lookalike. Among the many blondes auditioned was Catherine Hickland (Lindsay Rappaport).

Ilene Kristen was replaced as Georgina Whitman before the character became romantically involved with Bo Buchanan. That was the second time Kristen missed being Robert S. Woods's leading lady. Years before, he had auditioned to play Kristen's husband Frank Ryan on *Ryan's Hope*.

David Tom (Paul Cramer) might have landed the role of Pacey in the prime-time teen soap *Dawson's Creek* if he didn't look so much like the series star James Van Der Beek.

Dan Gauthier (Kevin Buchanan) came very close to landing the role of Michael Vaughn, the role Michael Vartan played on ABC's serialized spy saga *Alias*.

David O. Selznick himself auditioned Shepperd Strudwick (Victor Lord) to play Ashley Wilkes in *Gone With the Wind*.

After a successful reading with Jay Thomas and positive feedback from the producers, Hillary B. Smith (Nora Hanen) felt confident that she would be landing a leading role in the new CBS sitcom *Love & War*. At the last minute, the producers decided that they wanted a name actress in the lead and hired Susan Dey, who had just left *L.A. Law* and who lasted only one season before being replaced by Annie Potts. Smith herself would eventually costar in Gene Wilder's short-lived sitcom *Something Wilder*.

One of the first roles Nathan Fillion (Joey Buchanan) auditioned for after leaving *One Life to Live* was vampire-with-a-soul Angel on *Buffy the Vampire Slayer*. While he was not hired for that role, he did guest on *Buffy* during the last story arc, in which he played a demon-worshipping preacher. Around this same time, the character of Joey Buchanan (now played by Bruce Michael Hall) returned to Llanview as a minister.

Actors That Got Away

Ellen Holly (Carla Gray) recognized Morgan Freeman's immense talent when he came in to read for the role of Dr. Jack Scott, whom Holly's character Carla would eventually marry. She begged the producers to hire him.[23] Freeman landed a role on the soap opera *Another World* on his way to a film career that has so far earned him four Academy Award nominations and one Oscar (*Million Dollar Baby*).

While not all the actors *One Life to Live* failed to hire have gone on to Oscar gold, several have become names in and of themselves, especially on daytime.

Cameron Mathison, so popular as Ryan Lavery on *All My Children*, host of *I Wanna Be a Soap Star*, and competitor in *Dancing with the Stars*, auditioned for the role of Joey Buchanan. So did Brody Hutzler, most recently seen as Patrick Lockhart on *Days of Our Lives*.

Tracey Ross, who now plays Dr. Eve Russell on *Passions*, auditioned for the role of music company executive Jacara Principal.

For the past twenty-five years, Robert Newman has played Josh Lewis on *Guiding Light*. He landed the part while waiting to hear back about an under-five role he'd auditioned for at *One Life to Live*.

When soap newcomer Ty Treadway assumed the role of villainous Dr. Colin MacIver, he beat out some of daytime's bigger names, among them:

- Robert Kelker Kelly, who played both Sam Fowler and Shane Roberts on *Another World* as well as replacing Peter Reckell as Bo Brady on *Days of Our Lives*.
- Ian Buchanan (ex–Duke Lavery, *General Hospital*), who had also played a vampire on *Port Charles* and who would go on to play the sinister Dr. Greg Madden on *All My Children*.
- Laurence Lau, best known as *All My Children*'s good guy hero Greg Nelson.

Lau, who would later replace Kale Browne as Sam Rappaport, is a perfect example of those actors who didn't land the first *One Life* role for which they auditioned . . .

Before he was cast as cowboy Bo Buchanan, Robert S. Woods auditioned to play the far more sophisticated newspaperman Richard Abbott.

Renee Elise Goldsberry, whose character Evangeline Williamson was once romantically paired with RJ Gannon, had previously auditioned to play his niece Rachel.

If Melissa Archer (Natalie Buchanan) had landed the first role for which she tried out, Natalie's one-time rival Jen Rappaport, Archer would have been killed off by now.

Before Robin Christopher moved her character of Skye

Chandler from *All My Children* to *One Life to Live*, she read for the role of Gabrielle Medina with James DePaiva, who remembered her from the audition.

Jerry ver Dorn might have shown up in Llanview much earlier than 2006 if Procter & Gamble casting director Betty Rae hadn't convinced him to take the role of Ross Marler on *Guiding Light* rather than waiting to see if *One Life to Live* wanted him.

Distinguished Alumni

In 1994, Tommy Lee Jones won the Best Supporting Actor Oscar and Golden Globe for his role in *The Fugitive*, playing a U.S. Marshal hunting down Harrison Ford as a doctor wrongly accused of murder. Twenty years prior to that, Jones had played Mark Toland, a doctor who framed colleague Larry Wolek for murdering a patient. Jones once told *Soap Opera Digest* that his character had been morally upstanding until he gave the producers notice that he would be leaving the show.[24] A good sport, Jones agreed to come back for a two-week stint just so that his character could be killed off.

Among the suspects in Mark Toland's murder was his brother-in-law Tim Siegel, played by Tom Berenger. While Tim had not committed the murder, he was involved in the show's most controversial story line at the time: Tim, a Jewish law student, fell in love with Jenny Wolek (Katherine Glass), a novitiate nun. Like Tommy Lee Jones, Berenger ended his two-year run with a big death scene. Tim fell down those deadly stairs at Llanview Hospital and

Oscar winner Tommy Lee Jones played Dr. Mark Toland during the mid-1970s. Also pictured: Lee Warrick (center), who played Julie Siegel, and Jane Alice Brandon (right), who played Cathy Craig.

married Jenny on his hospital deathbed. Berenger's performance in Oliver Stone's Vietnam drama *Platoon* earned him an Oscar nomination and a Golden Globe as Best Supporting Actor.

Early in her acting career, Judith Light once vowed that she would never work on either a soap opera or a sitcom.[25] Talked into the role of housewife-turned-hooker Karen Wolek, Light won back-to-back Emmys. When she left the show in 1983, she seemed a shoo-in for a high-profile role in some prime-time drama, if not feature films. In Hollywood, Light discovered that her Emmys were not worth their weight in gold to casting directors because they were *only* Daytime Emmys. Although Light did film *Intimate Agony*, a movie of the week about the herpes epidemic, she found her biggest success in comedy, starring in the sitcom *Who's the Boss?* with Tony Danza. The series' popularity allowed Light to play the dramatic roles she handled so masterfully in MOWs such as *The Ryan White Story.* Recently Light has been recurring on both NBC's *Law & Order: Special Victims Unit,* as a judge, and on ABC's *Ugly Betty,* as a jailbird.

Julia Duffy, who filled in as an emergency replacement for Karen between Kathryn Breech and Judith Light, also found prime-time success in sitcoms, first *Newhart,* which earned her seven Emmy nominations, and later *Designing Women.*

At the same time that *Who's the Boss?* was ending its seven-year run on ABC, Light's on-screen sister Brynn Thayer (Jenny Wolek) was coming back to the network, joining the cast of the Andy Griffith legal drama *Matlock.* During the November sweeps of the 1991–92 season, Thayer had played a femme fatale who tried to seduce Matlock. In a move that must have confused many of the show's more ardent fans, by the end of that same season, Thayer was brought back, not as the femme fatale or even as another villain, but as Matlock's daughter.

The role of Jenny's abusive husband Brad Vernon was originated by Jameson Parker, who is best known from the long-running CBS detective series *Simon & Simon.*

While some actors, like Judith Light, discovered that soap opera work, even Emmy-winning soap opera work, can prejudice casting directors against a performer, Joe Lando (Jake Harrison) found his soap experience pivotal in landing the biggest role of his career. When CBS greenlit the Jane Seymour series *Dr. Quinn, Medicine Woman,* the producers saw tapes of Lando's work on *One Life to Live* and found his look and acting style a perfect fit for the character of backwoodsman Byron Sully. During Lando's last days at *One Life to Live*, CBS was sending over *Dr. Quinn* scripts for him to read.

Phylicia Rashad was brought onto *One Life to Live* as a love interest for Al Freeman Jr.'s Captain Ed Hall. Once Ed reunited with his ex-wife, Carla Gray (Ellen Holly), the story line dried up for Rashad's character Courtney, which turned out to be a blessing. She quickly landed a role in what would become the number one rated sitcom of the 1980s, *The Cosby Show*. During *Cosby's* first season, Rashad worked with Freeman, when he guested as Cliff Huxtable's (Bill Cosby) former track coach. After *The Cosby Show* ended its run, Rashad played Bill Cosby's wife again, in his follow-up sitcom, simply titled *Cosby*. Like *One Life to Live*, the *Cosby* sitcoms filmed in New York, which appealed to Rashad, who had been building up a Broadway career with musicals like *Dreamgirls* and *The Wiz*. In 2004, she became the first African-American to win the Tony Award for Best Actress, for the revival of *A Raisin in the Sun*.

At the age of twelve, future Oscar nominee Laurence Fishburne (*What's Love Got to Do With It*) joined the cast as Joshua West, a street kid adopted by police captain Ed Hall and his then new wife Carla. By age fourteen, Fishburne was working on the Francis Ford Coppola epic *Apocalypse Now*. His career continues to flourish thanks to megahits like *The Matrix* and its sequels.

In between Lillian Hayman's stints as Sadie Gray, Carla's mother and head of housekeeping at Llanview Hospital, the role was played by Esther Rolle, who would go on to play Bea Arthur's maid Florida on *Maude* before being spun off into her own sitcom, *Good Times*.

Ryan Phillippe's character Billy Douglas was introduced as the first gay teenager on daytime, with fanfare extending far beyond the soap press. After the homophobia story line ended, the writers didn't know what to do with Billy. The soap opera audience was not considered ready for a same-sex romance, so Billy was soon written off the show, which freed Phillippe up for what has become a successful career in film, including a pivotal role in the 2005 Best Picture winner *Crash* as well as two thumbs-up from Ebert and Roeper for *Flags of Our Fathers*. In the film *54*, Phillippe played a waiter dating an actress (Neve Campbell) from *All My Children*, who kept talking about how the soap opera was just her stepping stone to a big career.

One Life to Live introduced Irish-born Roma Downey to American TV audiences as Lady Johanna Leighton, whose father was the criminal mastermind holding Bo Buchanan hostage for months on end. Downey turned down the role of Xena: Warrior Princess to play the literally angelic Monica on the surprise hit *Touched by an Angel*.

When Blair Underwood (Bobby Blue) landed the role of high-priced attorney Jonathan Rollins on *L. A. Law*, one of the first people he called with the news was Erika Slezak, who as Viki and Niki had been both Bobby Blue's kidnap victim and his partner-in-crime. More recently, Underwood was seen in the ABC series *Dirty Sexy Money* and in bookstores as coauthor of the novel *Casanegra: A Tennyson Hardwick Novel*.

Before she was running in slow motion along the beach in the David Hasselhoff syndicated smash *Baywatch,* Yasmine Bleeth was caught between two Buchanan heirs: Asa's grandson Kevin Buchanan and Max Holden, whom Asa thought was his son.

In 1986, Bleeth's one-time boyfriend Richard Grieco came on the show as Rick Gardner, a skier with dreams of competing in the 1988 Winter Olympics. After leaving *One Life,* Grieco was cast in Fox's youth-oriented police show *21 Jump Street* and very quickly spun off into his own series, *Booker.*

Brandon Routh's career literally soared after being fired as Seth Anderson. Director Bryan Singer, looking for a relative unknown, cast Routh as the title character in *Superman Returns.* Routh, who had gone to a Halloween party the previous year dressed as the Man of Steel, signed on to the movie without even reading the script.

As a child, Hayden Panetierre, who plays the indestructible cheerleader on *Heroes,* played Sarah Roberts.

During the 1995–96 season, Ron Eldard (Blade) joined the cast of the top-rated drama *ER.* That same year, he played John Reilly in the Brad Pitt/Robert De Niro film *Sleepers.* Playing John as a child in the movie was Geoffrey Wigdor, who would join *One Life* as a pediatric AIDS patient the very next year.

Among the stars who have stopped briefly in Llanview on their way to greater fame have been Emmy winner Camryn Mannheim (*The Practice*) as Nora Hanen's rabbi; Oscar winner Kathy Bates as Evelyn Maddox; *One Tree Hill*'s Craig Sheffer as one of teenaged Cassie Callison's many suitors;

Dan Lauria, the father from *The Wonder Years,* as a thug named Gus Thompson; *Murphy Brown*'s Faith Ford as preppy Muffy Critchlow; Kelly McGillis as Glenda Livingston; *ER*'s Eriq La Salle as Mike Rivers; and Rainn Wilson from *The Office* as Casey Keegan.

From Llanview to Wisteria Lane

Shortly after Marcia Cross joined the show as archaeologist Kate Sanders, her leading man John Loprieno (Cord Roberts) realized that she was destined for a long and successful career. And right he was. Cross left the show after two years and guest-starred on prime-time hits like *Cheers* and *Seinfeld* before landing breakout roles on two decade-defining prime-time soaps: In the 1990s, she ran wild through *Melrose Place* as crazed doctor Kimberly Shaw, who in one cliffhanger blew up the entire complex; the new millennium finds her a tad more tightly wound, overwound some might say, as the picture-perfect housewife Bree Van Der Kamp Hodge on ABC's top-rated *Desperate Housewives*.

During the first season, Bree's husband was played by Steven Culp, one of the many actors who tackled the role of Dan Wolek.

Bree's homicidal mother-in-law during the third season was played by *Designing Women* star Dixie Carter, who subbed as Dorian Lord in the mid-seventies.

Tuc Watkins (who played David Vickers, one of Dorian's

many husbands) moved onto Wisteria Lane in 2007 as half of the show's first gay couple.

Nathan Fillion, whose Joey Buchanan was involved in a popular older woman/younger man love story with Dorian before she married David, also joined *Desperate Housewives* this season as the younger husband to Dana Delany. Fillion, who had a small role in *Saving Private Ryan,* joined the cast of *Two Guys and a Girl,* as a guy who got "the girl," and Joss Whedon's short-lived sci-fi series *Firefly* and its feature film adaptation *Serenity.*

I Do, I Do, I Do, I Do, I Do

In 1989, *All My Children*'s onetime supercouple Cliff and Nina married for a record-breaking fourth time. Had Tina Lord and Cord Roberts remained in Llanview, they might have broken Cliff and Nina's record. They were certainly on their way, having married and divorced three times. But it was Tina's brother Todd Manning and Cord's ex Blair Cramer, whom the writers never originally envisioned as a long-term couple, who broke the record. Based on their volatile history, Todd and Blair will probably break their own record in the not-too-distant future, maybe even by the time this book is published.

Marriage #1

Although Blair had developed a fondness for Todd, the discovery that he was actually Victor Lord's son and heir to millions made him marriage material in her mind. Unaware of his impending fortune, Todd couldn't imagine why Blair would be lying about being pregnant and proposed marriage. By the time Todd grew suspicious, Blair was actually expecting a baby. If not for the subsequent miscarriage, Todd might have gotten past the eventual revelations that Blair had known all along about his parentage and that she was lying about the baby. He divorced her, not realizing that she was pregnant again.

Marriage #2

Blair's second pregnancy made the divorce their shortest one to date. The two remarried in an elaborate though poorly attended wedding. Their second marriage seemed to end with Todd's apparent murder in Ireland. When Todd resurfaced alive a few months later, he was none too happy to see that his wife had already taken up with not just another man, but Patrick Thornhart, the same man for whom Todd had been mistaken when he was shot. Blair herself was none too happy when she learned of Todd's plan to run away with their daughter, Starr. Todd finalized their separation, divorcing Blair while she was comatose after a car accident.

After the divorce, Todd did something most unusual for him: He married a woman who wasn't Blair. He paid his lawyer, Téa Delgado, $5 million to marry him, giving him an advantage in the custody suit for Starr. In turn, Blair married someone who wasn't Todd, her first love, Max Holden.

Blair and Todd might have tried getting married again before 2001 if Todd hadn't left town for a couple of years. Their third trip down the aisle ended with Todd saying "No way" instead of "I do." The night before the wedding, he had spied Blair sleeping with her by this point ex-husband Max Holden, who (unbeknownst to Todd) had drugged her. Not only did Todd dump her at the altar, he also revealed that she was the one who had shot Max Holden in the back (a crime he helped her cover up).

Marriage #3

Blair married Todd later that year, unaware that he had given away their newborn son, whom he believed to be the child of Max Holden. Todd, who helped deliver the baby, convinced Blair that the child had died at birth. When Todd realized that he was the father, he took the baby back to Llanview and convinced Blair to adopt the little boy. Once Blair discovered that Jack was her child, the child Todd told her died, marriage number three came to a nasty finale.

Despite what many deemed his unforgivable sin, Todd and Blair grew close again while he was hiding her from the mob, which had killed Starr and Jack's nanny. A grateful Blair was walking down the aisle to make Todd her husband yet again when Sam Rappaport showed up with the not-so-dead nanny. Todd, it turned out, had concocted the whole mob scenario to win Blair back—and she was not charmed by the trouble to which he had gone.

Marriage #4

While Todd was presumed dead again, this time killed supposedly by Mitch Laurence, Blair fell in love with Walker Laurence, who had rescued her from his evil brother. By year's end, she married Walker, who turned out to be Todd post-plastic surgery. As soon as Todd's real identity was revealed, Blair ended the marriage. This time, though, she didn't need to file for divorce; because Todd had married her under a false identity, the union qualified for an annulment.

After three divorces, one annulment, and several aborted attempts to get through a ceremony, Blair wasn't surprised when Todd didn't show up for their latest wedding. She didn't realize for some time that he'd been kidnapped by Margaret Cochran, a former employee harboring a fatal attraction for him.

Marriage #5

Todd believed that marrying Blair for a fifth time would convince a judge that he could provide a stable home for his son Tommy during the custody battle with Marcie and Michael McBain. Blair demanded $5 million for her hand in marriage, the same deal Todd offered Téa Delgado, who married Todd during his custody battle with Blair.

While people may not understand why Blair keeps going back to Todd, you do have to give her credit for her sheer nerve. Few other women getting married for the seventh time, the fifth to the same man, would actually put on a white dress.

3
Tales from Backstage

First Day on the Job

Upon receiving his first script, Phil Carey (Asa Buchanan), who had been working in prime time, asked how many pages he needed to learn. When he heard "all of them," he called up his wife and told her, "Don't unpack."[26]

Jessica Tuck (Megan Gordon) was so nervous her first day that she literally could not speak—a fact cast mate James DePaiva (Max Holden) never let her forget.

Although Timothy Gibbs had worked on two soap operas (*Santa Barbara* and *Another World*) before taking over the role of Kevin Buchanan, he was nervous his very first day in Llanview, so nervous that his knees were shaking, so much so that leading lady Laura Koffman (Cassie Callison) worried he would not be able to carry her over the threshold as called for in the scene.

Audiences first saw David Chisum as Miles Laurence as a facially disfigured patient during Spencer Truman's (Paul Satterfield) videotaped will. For those few minutes of screen time, the makeup artists spent approximately four hours applying prosthetics to Chisum's face.

What's My Line?

Teleprompters were removed from the *OLTL* studios in 1988. Michael Storm (Dr. Larry Wolek) was thrilled to see them go since he blamed them for too many actors not looking him in the eye during their scenes.[27] Taping an hour-long show a day forces some actors to get creative on how they memorize their lines or at least how they keep them close at hand.

For the actors, the library at Llanfair remains one of the more popular sets because it offers them so many places to hide their scripts. At least one can usually be found underneath the seat cushions of the couch. The cutlery drawer in the kitchen at Llanfair offers another popular hiding spot.

Ernest Graves (Victor Lord) and his on-screen daughter Lynn Benesch (Meredith Wolek) loved scenes that took place on the terrace outside the library at Llanfair because they could tape their lines to the fake trees. The two of them would cut their scripts into strips, which they would then tape to the leaves. They worked out a system where Graves would use the higher branches and Benesch the lower because he was taller.

James DePaiva (Max Holden) would occasionally head down to the lobby of the ABC building to memorize his script. The noise—both the foot traffic in and out of the building as well as the street traffic outside—actually helped his concentration.

Linda Dano (Rae Cummings) always waited until an hour before taping a scene to memorize her lines. Doing so, she believed, made her a more attentive listener on the set. It also drove the directors crazy during rehearsal.[28]

Mark Arnold (Rob Coronal) would memorize a week's worth of scripts at a time.

Jacqueline Courtney (Pat Ashley) would write lines down on her hands. That usually worked fine—except when she was doing a scene with Phil Carey (Asa Buchanan), who loved to wet his hand and shake Courtney's, intentionally smudging the lines she'd written down.

Jessica Tuck's (Megan Gordon) parrot Puck would sit quietly on her head or shoulder while she ran through her lines.

When Bruce Michael Hall joined the cast as Joey Buchanan, his on-screen uncle Robert S. Woods (Bo Buchanan) gave him some profound advice about learning his lines: "Almost as important as remembering the words is getting them in the right order."

Accidents Will Happen

lorencia Lozano's (Téa Delgado) dressing room once caught on fire, but it was extinguished before any real damage was done. For the most part, though, the actors tend to save their accidents, especially their fires, for the set.

Fiona Hutchison's (Gabrielle Medina) hair caught fire while she was filming a romantic, candelit love scene with Nicholas Walker, who was playing Max Holden at the time.

James DePaiva (the original and final Max Holden) injured himself while taping a less than romantic scene with Kassie DePaiva (Blair Cramer). To capture the lust-driven foundation of their affair, the actors were directed to play their sex scenes rough rather than tender. A little too rough, as it turned out. During one such scene, the DePaivas fell over a sofa, leaving James with a bloody lip.

Robert S. Woods (Bo Buchanan) loves motorcycles so much he couldn't resist hopping onto one during a chase scene. When he pulled up on the handlebars to do a wheelie, the bike flipped over backward. Jean Arley, who was producing at the time, didn't realize that Woods himself was riding on the bike. She assumed that the bike had flipped over onto a professional stuntman, someone trained not to get hurt. Arley was horrified to discover the show's star lying on the ground. After that mishap, Woods was banned from riding motorcycles.

Near the beginning of their romance, Nash Brennan (Forbes March) took Jessica's alternate personality Tess (Bree Williamson) on a Rollerblading date. They were still on wheels when Nash brought her home to his apartment. Showing off his Rollerblading skills, March quickly wound up flat on his rear end.

During the Badhra Diamond story line, Tuc Watkins (David Vickers) got so caught up in his character's scheme to steal the jewel away from Dorian (Robin Strasser), he walked right into a coffee table. The accident, he told *Soap Opera Digest*, added a new dimension to Watkins's portrayal. He no longer envisioned David as a suave and sometimes ruthless con artist. He reimagined him as more comic than menacing, playing him from then on as a Cary Grant wannabe.

A fight scene between Joey (Don Jeffcoat) and Kelly (Gina Tognoni) called for Kelly to punch Joey in the stomach. Wanting the scene to look as realistic as possible, Jeffcoat told Tognoni to really hit him, not to pull her punch at the last second. He wasn't expecting the former beauty pageant winner to throw such a powerful punch.

Hillary B. Smith (Nora Hanen) and Ty Treadway (Troy MacIver) were nearly killed during a scene in which Nora's car veered off a bridge and Troy jumped into the water to rescue her. The pool of water in which the scene was filmed was metal and had become electrified during the taping.

They were saved only by the fact that the pool was lined with a rubber mat. Still, both Hillary B. Smith and Treadway felt a shock. After the problem was corrected, the two were sent back into the pool to retape the scene.

Although one thing probably had nothing to do with the other, a blackout hit New York City as Kamar de los Reyes and Bree Williamson were taping one of Antonio and Jessica's love scenes.

Getting into Character

Anthony and Victor Biase, the twin brothers who played Cord and Tina's son CJ as a baby, were born actors. Even at age one, they were calling John Loprieno (Cord) "Dada." And whenever they heard the *One Life to Live* theme song, they immediately crawled right over to the TV. The adult actors on the show have developed their own methods for getting into character and little tricks to make a scene work.

When Judith Light landed the role of Karen Wolek, the housewife who turned to prostitution, Light literally hit the streets. She went out to talk to real-life hookers working in New York. She not only talked to them, she also observed them in action.

During her 1995 multiple personality story line, Erika Slezak found Princess, the frightened little girl, the most difficult of Viki's alternate personalities to play. Director Gary Tomlin told Slezak to remember that little children, because of their size, are always looking up at the adult to whom they are speaking. That one physical detail gave

Judith Light (pictured here with Gerald Anthony, who played Marco Dane), observed and interviewed real-life hookers to prepare for her character Karen Wolek's prostitution story line.

Slezak the perspective she needed to make the Princess scenes work.[29]

According to *Soap Opera Digest*, Robin Strasser (Dorian Lord) prefers that her leading men do not wear cologne, especially during the love scenes. She also hates to be complimented on her performance during rehearsals; she's afraid of jinxing the actual taping.

As much as Stephen Markle loved playing the hard-drinking newspaper reporter Mel Hayes, the chain-smoking aspect of the character tested his willpower. Two years before coming to *One Life*, Markle himself had quit smoking.

After Clint Buchanan had been blinded, Clint Ritchie

did not want to worry about his eyes focusing on people and objects that Clint should not be able to see. He asked the prop department for dark sunglasses he could hide his eyes behind.[30]

Taping Megan Gordon's hospital-bed death in 1992, the director tied a string around Jessica Tuck's big toe. One tug instructed Tuck to hold her breath because the camera was zooming in for a close-up. Two tugs let her know that she could start breathing again.

Kentucky-born Kassie DePaiva was told to lose her Southern twang when she took over the role of Blair Cramer. The producers wanted to distinguish her from North Carolina native Susan Batten (Luna Moody), who would be Blair's rival for the affections of Max Holden (James DePaiva).

When Bree Williamson first took over as Jessica Buchanan, she needed to adjust her Canadian accent, such as stop pronouncing "about" like "a-boot."

Sometimes, it seems, an actor can get a little *too* into character . . .

Despite the age difference, viewers never suspected that Jason Webb (Mark Brettschneider) was faking his interest in Dorian Lord (then played by Elaine Princi). So convincingly passionate was Brettschneider that the directors actually told him to tone down the love scenes.

Shortly after Dr. Michael McBain broke his leg, so too did Nathaniel Marston, who played him. While a noble effort, a more attentive-to-detail actor might have broken the correct leg. Marston broke his right leg, whereas Michael had broken his left, necessitating a little revisionist history:

Viewers saw Michael suddenly sporting a cast on the opposite leg.

After the plot twist in which Lana McClain was impregnated by Brad Vernon (Jameson Parker), Jacklyn Zeman
actually suffered from psychosomatic morning sickness.

Real-life pregnancies, whether written into the story
line or not, present actresses with a whole host of added
challenges . . .

Tari Signor (Margaret Cochran) told *Soap Opera Digest*
that she found it rather amusing how she herself was so far
along in her own pregnancy during the scenes in which
Margaret tied Todd down to a bed, forcing him to impreg-
nate her.

When Erika Slezak was expecting her first child (son Michael), the pregnancy was written into her story line. Gordon
Russell, head writer at the time, promised Slezak that he
would not jinx her real baby with any on-screen dramatics.
Viki's son Joey would not suffer from any life-threatening
health crises or be kidnapped the way his older brother Kevin
had been. (In fact, Joey was the only one of Viki's children
not kidnapped shortly after being born.) Before Slezak left
on her maternity leave, she played out the scene where Viki
gave birth. The actress's obstetrician warned her against
pushing during the scene, even against fake pushing.

Shortly after Kassie DePaiva announced that she was
pregnant, Blair discovered that she was carrying Patrick
Thornhart's child. Unlike DePaiva, Blair was not thrilled
by the new life growing inside her. The dialogue often demanded that DePaiva scream how much she hated the baby
and didn't want it. As soon as the scene ended, DePaiva
would talk to her stomach, assuring the child inside her,

"Mommy's just pretending." Even more difficult for De-Paiva, she was still pregnant when Blair suffered a miscarriage.[31] Part of the hospital bed mattress was removed so that, while lying in it, the eight months pregnant DePaiva's stomach would look flatter.

He Who Laughs Last

One of the biggest practical jokers on the set has been Robert S. Woods (Bo Buchanan), who plays the *NYPD Blue* theme song on a little recorder whenever Bo arrests someone. Woods also hides up on the catwalk over the sets, where he can drop fake spiders onto cast mates during rehearsals. He'll also tie strings around different props, like the telephone, so he can hoist them up mid-scene.

Woods is not afraid to go after anyone. While Erika Slezak (Viki Lord Davidson) was cleaning her dressing room, Woods took all the items she had placed outside her door, tagged them with prices, and lined them up along the hallway. He then taped up signs directing cast and crew to a "Star Garage Sale."

In perhaps his bravest stunt, he rigged Phil Carey's (Asa Buchanan) cigar to blow up in his face.

Robert Gentry and Kim Zimmer spent the better part of 1983 as Giles Morgan and Echo di Savoy, a brother and sister who blamed Clint Buchanan for their mother's death. For Zimmer and Gentry's last day, the two showed up dressed as each other. Gentry put on a dress while Zimmer taped on a fake mustache.

For one on-set joke, James DePaiva took his cue straight from Max Holden. To put Megan Gordon (Jessica Tuck) in her place, Max filled her drink with salt. DePaiva did the same thing to the glass Tuck would be drinking from on-screen.

Right before a scene in which Lindsay Rappaport (Catherine Hickland) and Clint Buchanan (Clint Ritchie) were to be eating Chinese food, Hickland slipped a risqué fortune into the cookie that Clint broke open.

Patricia Elliott (Renee Divine) and on-screen son Mark Derwin (Ben Davidson) would gross out the crew by pulling each other into a passionate kiss after the cameras finished rolling on one of their mother-and-son scenes.

Mark Derwin (Ben Davidson) not only played his share of jokes on the set, he was on the receiving end of a few. One of the best was played on him by the costume department, which convinced Derwin that Ben would be going into hiding dressed as a woman. Derwin was dolled up in a dress, wig, and makeup, then sent up to the producers' office for approval. Derwin wound up interrupting a production meeting to show off Ben's feminine side, which he learned was not intended for any upcoming story line.

Hair Care

Gina Tognoni (Kelly Cramer) spent more time than anyone else in the chair, mainly because she would spend so much time chatting that her hair rarely stayed still long enough for a decent cutting.

Heather Tom (Kelly Cramer) could not bring her dog along when she was getting her hair done. The dog would bark and growl at anyone who came near Tom with a pair of scissors or even a comb.

Roxy Balsom's (Ilene Kristen) outlandish look requires the hairdressers to keep a hundred hairpieces on hand just for her character. They take up an entire shelf in the studio's hairdressing closet.

While the show does not stock quite as many for Dorian Lord, Robin Strasser has taken to naming the ones they use for her.

Timothy Stickney (RJ Gannon) was the first black contract player on daytime to sport dreadlocks. Stickney was wearing them before they came into vogue, and he credits them with helping him scare people out of their seats on the subway.

Roger Howarth (Todd Manning) grew out his mane to its signature length at the request of his son, who wanted to see his dad with long hair.

Whenever Kassie DePaiva has wanted to cut her hair more than an inch or two, the style change has always been incorporated on-screen into Blair's story line. At one point, Blair chopped off her hair because she didn't want to look like Marty Saybrooke. Another time, rival Skye Chandler chopped it off while Blair slept. During the taping of that scene, the scissors were shaking in actress Robin Christopher's hands. Christopher was terrified not only of cutting DePaiva's hair for real but knowing that it had to be done right the first time.

When Nora Hanen (Hillary B. Smith) imagined that husband Bo was having an affair with her assistant Georgie (Jennifer Bransford), she took a razor to her hair. Before taping the scene, Smith visited her own stylist, who cut her hair and added in extensions. Viewers then saw Smith cutting off the extensions, not her own hair.

During Nora's first brain tumor story line, Smith shaved a three-by-three-inch patch in the back of her head. *One Life to Live* never showed the bald patch, opting instead to dress Nora in head bands. The next time that Nora was slated to battle a brain tumor, Smith agreed to completely shave her head bald. Luckily, she held off doing so, as head writer Claire Labine, who was penning that story line, left and the story line was shelved.

Before Viki was wheeled into brain surgery, Erika Slezak spent more than an hour in the chair having her hair plastered down and a bald wig applied over it—only to have the scene cut. Slezak did, however, get to go bald on-screen during Viki's breast cancer story line.

Forbes March (Nash Brennan) hated the long hair that the producers wanted to distinguish him as a rebel.[32] He hated it so much that he started a backstage petition, pressuring the producers into letting him cut his hair.

Costume Fittings and Fitting Costumes

When the character of Bo Buchanan was first introduced on the show, Robert S. Woods was allowed
to pick out the Western-themed apparel he'd be wearing on
camera.

Right before shooting his first scene with Phil Carey (Asa
Buchanan), Anthony George (Will Vernon) teased him
about Asa's fur-collared overcoat, likening it to something
Joan Crawford would wear.

When Clint Ritchie (Clint Buchanan) debuted on the
show, the costume department told him that the producers
wanted him to wear dress shoes, not cowboy boots. Ritchie,
who intended to wear his boots, suggested that the camera-
men not film his feet.

The costume department didn't score any more points
with Ritchie when they offered him his choice of fluores-
cent swimming trunks to wear during Clint's first scene at
the health club. Ritchie, who used to manage a gym, opted
to wear his own sweatpants. He also grabbed a spray bottle
and turned it on himself to simulate sweat, something he

thought Clint should be doing at the gym. In doing so, he started a trend. In his next health club scene, he noticed that all the actors were spraying water on themselves before taping.

Robin Strasser (Dorian Lord) taught both her on-screen daughter Laura Koffman (Cassie Cramer) and niece Gina Tognoni (Kelly Cramer) the proper way to walk down the marble staircase in Dorian's front hall in high heels without making a sound.

The usually refined Megan Gordon (Jessica Tuck) developed a second personality, a rather loud character who called herself Ruby Bright. Ruby's costume consisted of a curly brunette wig and a leopard-print dress. The first time Tuck tried on the outfit, not even the crew recognized her.

The costumers would often take Hillary B. Smith with them when they went out to buy Nora Hanen's wardrobe, needing Smith there to try the outfits on. Trusting their judgment as to what looked best on her, Smith would buy for herself any suit that the costumers picked out for Nora.

The wedding of Luna Moody and Max Holden was scheduled to begin taping on Monday morning at 9:00 sharp. The fact that Luna's wedding dress had not arrived until 5:00 the previous Friday afternoon would not have created a panic had the dress not arrived in pieces. The costume department worked through the weekend, stitching the dress together and then applying the sequins, the last of which were being glued on at five minutes until nine.

Mark Goddard wanted a memorable exit for the character of Ted Clayton, Tina's presumed father and the head of a counterfeiting organization. Goddard suggested to the writers that Ted meet his end dressed as a woman, and that

When Luna Moody (Susan Batten) married Max Holden (James DePaiva), the wedding dress was finished only five minutes before taping was scheduled to begin.

he did. He was electrocuted while trying to escape town disguised as a woman. The image of Goddard in drag sparked the writers' imagination; they suddenly wanted to keep Ted around, but Goddard told *Soap Opera Digest* that one day in drag was all he could take.

Postcards from the Road

In 1970, *One Life to Live* had been praised for the way it incorporated a real-life drug rehabilitation center into its story line. Since then, the producers have found that the right location can often add a needed touch of realism to an existing story line. When Brad Vernon (Steve Fletcher) was sent to prison, the show enhanced the bleakness of his situation by taping the scenes in an actual New Jersey prison.

Unfortunately, the daytime budget didn't always allow for first-class accommodations. When Robert S. Woods (Bo Buchanan) and Jacqueline Courtney (Pat Ashley) traveled to Paris, they went with a limited number of crew members. Woods and Courtney were required not only to do their own hair and makeup, they had to lug their costumes out of the backseat of a station wagon, which they drove from scene to scene.

Five years later, the show sent Woods back to Europe as Bo, specifically to Venice. This time, a number of cast members went along, including Phil Carey (Asa Buchanan) and Gerry Anthony (Marco Dane), who fell in love with the city, deeming it one of the most beautiful he'd ever seen. Unlike the Paris remote, Venice emphasized action and adventure, revolving around Asa's kidnapping. Despite the expanded budget and higher production values, executive producer Paul Rauch named the Venice remote as the least successful story line in his years on the show.[33] To give the story line a little "authentic" local flavor, the show hired Miss Teenage Italy Fabiano Udenio, a young woman who had actually been born in Argentina, where the show would head two years down the road.

While the studio lights can warm up the sets to a little less than comfortable temperatures at times, the 1987 trip to Argentina found the show's actors working in 120-degree weather. Because of the intense heat, cast and crew were dropping like flies. A nurse was hired to look after them. Even John Loprieno (Cord Roberts) fell victim to heat prostration. James DePaiva (Max Holden), still relatively new on the show and terrified of being fired, was feeling ill himself but refused to let it show.[34] Sick as he was, he carried out all the story line's physical demands, including hiking up a mountain. He waited to collapse until he'd returned to New York City.

The first time Robin Strasser left *One Life to Live*, Dorian Lord had been appointed ambassador to Mendorra. Years later, Megan Gordon's ex-lover Prince Raymond (Robert Westenberg) from Mendorra traveled to Llanview to be treated for his impending blindness. His evil brother, Prince Roland (Joseph Kolinski), took advantage of Raymond's health problems to undermine his ascension to the throne. The producers planned to film the conclusion to this royal battle on location and chose Salzburg, Austria, to

"play" Mendorra. (Four years prior, the conclusion to David Renaldi's spy saga was filmed in Vienna.) The Salzburg
remote proved to be the show's most expensive location
shoot. Paul Rauch had thought that the Austrian location
would lure Strasser back to the show, even for a short stint,
but it didn't.[35] The story's daring escape sequence—Bo,
Megan, and Sarah (Jensen Buchanan) skiing down a
mountain—faced a major obstacle: An unusually warm
patch of weather had left the mountain a touch bare. Rauch
hired the biggest snow machine in all of Europe to supply
the snow he needed to make the scene work.

In 1982, mad scientist Ivan Kipling kidnapped Karen
Wolek and took her to his plantation in San Carlos, South
America. Like Mendorra, San Carlos existed only in the
world of *One Life to Live*. Although San Carlos was located in South America, the producers filmed the outdoor
jungle scenes in Silver Springs, Florida. Michael Storm
(whose character, Dr. Larry Wolek, had recently fallen back
in love with ex-wife Karen) was initially thrilled to be playing the hero in the sort of action-adventure story line that
was becoming so popular on daytime.[36] His thrill turned
to trepidation on the first day of shooting, when the stage
manager handed out flea and tick collars. At one point during the shoot, Judith Light (Karen) wandered into a patch
of quicksand. When the crew noticed that she was sinking
into the ground, they immediately pulled her out.

No sooner did *One Life* return from Florida than it hit
the road again. In 1982, CBS debuted the political soap
opera *Capitol*, set in a fictional town outside Washington,
D.C. The show was scheduled for the 2:30–3:00 time slot,
opposite the second half of *One Life to Live*. According to

Soap Opera Digest, the producers of *One Life to Live* hoped to undermine the debut with a capital location shoot of its own. Asa, Bo, and Viki were sent down to Washington, D.C., for a tale of political intrigue.

When Clint Buchanan traveled into the Wild West, the show headed out to Arizona, to Old Tucson, which had been built specifically for the 1940s Western *Arizona.* The John Wayne classic *Rio Lobo* and several episodes of the TV series *Bonanza* had been shot there as well. John Loprieno, who would be playing Cody in the Wild West story line, was sent ahead to learn how to ride a horse hard and fast, the way it would have been done in the 1880s. The footage of Loprieno's most impressive riding, however, wound up on the cutting room floor.

The Ivy League's Princeton University filled in as Llanview U during the Music Box Killer story line, where Dr. Stephen Haver, the serial strangler, was not only targeting the coeds but also teaching a course.

Central Park has provided the backdrop for numerous story lines through the years, among them Viki's second marriage to Joe Riley; Bo Buchanan's romantic picnic with Didi O'Neill (Barbara Treutelaar); Starr Manning's kidnapping; and Asa's Cleopatra-themed wedding to Alex Olanov. While Alex's skimpy Egyptian wedding dress looked amazing, it provided little protection against the weather for actress Tonja Walker, who caught a cold taping the outdoor scenes. During the 2002 week of live shows, the cameras headed back to Central Park for an ambitious remote despite threats that cast members from *As the World Turns* would be streaking through the scene.

Big Love—Asa Style

E ven when you factor in the intentional bigamy, trigamy actually (juggling three wives at one point), Asa Buchanan ranks as the most married man on daytime television.

1. Olympia Buchanan
    This was Asa's first and longest marriage. Granted, Olympia spent the majority of that thirty-plus-year marriage banished to Europe after cheating on Asa and killing her lover.

1b. Pamela Oliver
    Posing as Captain Jeb Stuart, Asa married school-teacher Pamela Oliver on the island of Malakeva and visited whenever the urge struck. Viewers did not meet Pamela until the mid-1980s.

1c. Samantha Vernon
    Asa was nearly shot to death by Olympia while ex-changing vows with Sam. Olympia's subsequent death

(while trying to shoot Asa yet again, this time at his masquerade party) did free him up to marry Samantha for real, but she didn't want anything more to do with him.

2. Delila Ralston
   The niece of Yancey Ralston, the lover Olympia killed, Delila married Asa mainly because she couldn't have Bo, whom she believed to be her cousin. As soon as the truth came out, that Bo was really a Buchanan and no relation to her, Delila left Asa. While she did marry Bo, the marriage didn't last too long. She eventually wound up happily married to Asa's nephew Rafe.

3. Becky Lee Abbott
   Like Delila, Becky Lee was also in love with Bo—not only in love with him, but pregnant with his baby. Determined that the child would be raised a Buchanan, Asa pressured Becky Lee into marriage, then fell in love with her. After a plane crash, an amnesiac Becky fell in love with another man. Although her memory eventually returned, her love for Asa did not.

4. Pamela Oliver
   The illegal second wife became the legal fourth. Furious at Asa's deception, Pamela tricked him into marriage by pretending to be on her deathbed. Beating Asa at his own game ultimately proved more satisfying to her than marriage to him.

5. Renee Divine
    The true love of Asa's life. It would take Asa a few
    tries to get this one right. The marriage fell apart when
    Renee hid the truth that Max Holden was not his
    biological son.

6. Blair Cramer
    In love with Max Holden when she married Asa,
    Dorian Lord's niece Blair actually made love to Max
    on top of her own wedding gown shortly before the
    ceremony. Desperate to be a wealthy widow, Blair once
    withheld Asa's heart medication—a trick she obviously
    picked up from Aunt Dorian.

7. Alex Olanov
    Family and friends could not believe that Asa would
    marry this former federal agent turned mob queen
    with a one-time fatal attraction for Asa's son Bo.
    Twice, no less! Mob boss Carlo Hesser's return from
    the dead invalidated his "widow" Alex's marriage to
    Asa, but Asa remarried her once she divorced Carlo.
    Eventually, Alex would divorce Asa to remarry Carlo,
    who wasn't as willing as Asa to take Alex for his bride
    a second time. [Alex would try to blackmail Asa into a
    third wedding, but that wedding would end up with
    Alex married to a drunken hobo.]

8. Renee Divine
    If marrying Alex twice had been a mistake, Asa did get
    something right remarrying Renee. On their wedding
    day, Renee confessed a secret: Years ago, she'd given

birth to Asa's son, then gave the child up for adoption. Asa's nemesis Max Holden once again passed himself off as Asa's son and once again Renee and Asa's marriage fell apart when the truth about Max came out.

9. Gabrielle Medina
   A fake marriage from the outset, Asa and Max Holden's ex-lover Gabrielle wed as part of an elaborate scheme to send Max to prison. The plan might have succeeded had Gabrielle not fallen back in love with her ex.

10. Rae Cummings
    Asa came out of a few marriages hating his wife (Olympia, Blair, Alex), but he only went into one hating the woman. His one-time court-appointed shrink, Rae had tape-recorded Asa's various confessions and blackmailed him into a short-term marriage.

11. Renee Divine
    Fittingly, the true love of Asa's life, Renee Divine became his last wife.

Expecting the Unexpected: Llanview's More Unorthodox Pregnancies

||||||||||||||||||||||||||||||||||||||||||||||||||||||||||||||||||||||||||||||||||||||||||||||||||||||||||||||||||||||||||||||||||||||||||||||||||||||||||||||||||||||||||||||||||||||||||||||

J ared Banks showed up at the reading of Asa Buchanan's will, claiming to be the long-lost son to whom Asa
alluded on the tape. The real heir, who doesn't know it, is
the slightly more seasoned con artist David Vickers. Years
ago, Asa's own son Clint discovered Cord Roberts, a son
he'd never known. Such surprise children and impostors account for a significant voting population in a town like
Llanview. For a woman to discover such a long-lost child,
not just one she'd given up for adoption, but one she never
realized she gave birth to in the first place . . . ? Pregnancies
like that are what drive obstetricians like the infamous Dr.
Balsom to join bizarre cults.

Viki Buchanan

Under hypnosis, Viki Buchanan realized that her party girl
alter Niki Smith had emerged far earlier than anyone had ever
suspected. Niki had gained control of Viki's mind during the
entire nine months Viki was carrying daughter Megan. Once
Viki regained control, her control freak father, who had given

the baby away, paid a hypnotist to erase any memories Viki may have had related to the pregnancy; in their place the magician also implanted memories of a typical senior year in high school.

Viki Buchanan (Take Two)

Viki gave birth not just to one daughter she didn't know about but two. Her obstetrician, Dr. Balsom, who belonged to Mitch Laurence's cult, never told her that she was carrying twins. The second baby, Natalie, the not-so-good doctor brought home to his drunken wife, Roxie. Making this pregnancy completely twisted, the two girls, Natalie and Jessica, had been fathered by different men: Viki's husband Clint was Natalie's father, while Mitch Laurence had impregnated Viki with Jessica when he drugged and raped her.

Jessica Buchanan

Like mother, like daughter, one might say. Not only was the paternity of baby Brennan in doubt, so too was her *maternity*. No one knew whether or not Brennan had been conceived during a period when Jessica's alternate personality Tess was in control. No one knew until the DNA test proved that Tess's lover Nash Brennan was the father.

Tina Roberts

While there were no strange circumstances surrounding the conception of CJ, Tina Roberts deserves credit for one of the sturdiest pregnancies in daytime history. A pregnant Tina not only survived a trip over the Iguazu Falls in Argentina, she then delivered a healthy baby boy, aptly named Milagro (Spanish for "miracle") by the natives.

Delila Ralston

After a pregnant Sam Garretson was left brain dead, her best friend Delila Ralston offered to become a surrogate mother for the baby inside her. Delila wound up not only becoming mother to Sam's baby but also a second wife to Sam's widowed husband, Rafe.

Keri Reynolds

In one of the show's more convoluted tales of embryo transfer, law professor Keri Reynolds offered to carry the baby when her mother, Liz, announced that she was pregnant with a most unexpected and inconvenient baby. It was an especially generous offer on Keri's part since her mother was pregnant by Keri's boyfriend Antonio. Ultimately, the embryo transfer did not take, because Keri, as it turned out, was already pregnant by the incredibly fertile Antonio.

Margaret Cochran

While soap opera children, like Jessica Buchanan, are occasionally conceived in rape, it's not usually the man who has been victimized. The obsessive Margaret Cochran kidnapped Todd Manning, tied him to a bed, and forced him into sex under threat of killing his beloved Blair.

4
Getting Personal

Fun Facts About the Actors

Namesakes

Robin Strasser's (Dorian Lord) mother honored the end of World War II by giving Strasser, who was born on May 7, the unusual three-names-in-one middle name "Victory in Europe."

Bree Williamson (Jessica Buchanan) was named after Kate Jackson's character on *Charlie's Angels*, Sabrina "Bree" Duncan.

Although Farah Fath (Gigi Morasco) spells her name differently, she was named after Jackson's costar in the series, Farrah Fawcett.

Robin Christopher's (Skye Chandler) mother was lying in her hospital bed after giving birth, trying to think what to name her baby girl, when a robin landed on the sill outside her window.

Ty (short for Tyrus) Treadway (Drs. Colin and Troy MacIver) was named after the baseball great Ty (Tyrus) Cobb.

Bree Williamson, who plays Jessica Buchanan, was named after Kate Jackson's character on *Charlie's Angels*. Also pictured: Jerry ver Dorn, who plays Clint Buchanan.

Odd Jobs

Lee Patterson (Joe Riley and Tom Dennison) had one of the more eclectic pre-soap résumés: He prospected for gold, drew cartoons, and caddied for legendary comedian Jack Benny.

Mark Derwin, whose character Ben changed Viki's last name from Carpenter to Davidson, once worked as a carpenter.

Robert S. Woods, who cut many a rug throughout Bo's romance with Nora Hanen (Hillary B. Smith), didn't need too much instruction. In his younger days, he taught ball-room dancing.

Patricia Elliott, whose character Renee Divine hails from Reno, actually worked in Reno, but not in a brothel, at Harrah's casino. Elliott would carry around fifty pounds of coins for the gamblers playing the slot machines.

Karen Witter (Tina Lord) conducted hot air balloon rides.

Paul Satterfield (Dr. Spencer Truman) spent one summer bucking hay on a farm. As if it weren't hard enough tossing around hundred-pound bundles of hay in temperatures that sometimes climbed past the hundred mark, Satterfield happened to be allergic to hay.

Nathan Purdee, who played D.A. Hank Gannon, put himself through college working as a bounty hunter.

Timothy Stickney (RJ Gannon) used to run a comic book store. A fan, he didn't mind being paid in comic books.

Justis Bolding (Sarah Roberts), who once dreamed about training tigers for a living, wound up training dogs instead.

Talbot Huddleston's sins in Llanview were legion: He hired prostitutes, ran down a little boy, and murdered a doctor. Byron Sanders, who played Talbot, actually modeled as Jesus Christ for Salvador Dalí's painting *Crucifixion,* which now hangs in the Museum of Modern Art.

Wortham Krimmer's (Reverend Andrew Carpenter) job managing a San Francisco apartment complex involved not only the usual tasks of changing lightbulbs and fixing toilets, but also a little bit of ghost hunting. Prior to Krimmer taking over the job, a tenant had burned to death in one of the apartments. Another couple, who lived in the building and had known him, insisted that his spirit was trying to make contact with them. The couple would wake Krimmer up in the middle of the night to roam the apartment complex with them, looking for the ghost.

Education

Margaret Klenck (Edwina Lewis) studied mime in Paris with Marcel Marceau's teacher despite the fact that she had not yet mastered fluency in spoken French.

Brenda Brock, who played nurse Brenda McGillis, had actually studied nursing at the University of Texas.

Sherri Saum, who played law professor Keri Reynolds, had herself enrolled in John Jay College of Criminal Justice with the intention of becoming an FBI agent.

Jessica Tuck (Megan Gordon) majored in psychology at Yale.

A biology major at UC, Irvine, Karen Witter (Tina Lord) intended to study the biochemical roots of schizophrenia.

As if memorizing lines were not enough homework for Brittany Underwood (Langston Wilde), she is majoring in biology at Manhattanville College.

When Patricia Mauceri (Carlotta Vega) attended the Juilliard School, her classmates included future Tony winner Patti Lupone and future Oscar winners Kevin Kline and Robin Williams.

Pets

Melissa Archer (Natalie Buchanan) owns cats even though she is allergic to them.

A former stand-up comedian, Nathan Purdee (Hank Gannon) once traded away his monologue and joke book for a dog he named Caesar after Caesar's Palace in Las Vegas.

Patricia Mauceri (Carlotta Vega) has owned not just snakes but two of the deadliest breeds, boa constrictor and python.

Catherine Hickland (Lindsay Rappaport) once owned a pet skunk.

When she was growing up, Andrea Evans (Tina Lord) owned a bird, a guinea pig, a cat, and a dog—all of whom slept in the same bed with her.

Beauty Pageants

Tonja Walker (Alex Olanov), the 1979 Miss Teen All American, was also Miss Maryland the following year and made it to the top ten finalists in the Miss USA pageant.

At age five, Tammy Amerson (Mari Lynn Dennison) was named Miss Hemisphere. She also won four other national titles, with prizes such as a car she was far too young to drive. Her mother made all the dresses she wore to competitions.

Being born in Missouri did not keep Gina Tognoni (Kelly Cramer) from being named Miss Rhode Island Teen or Miss Rhode Island All-American Teen.

Kimberlin Brown (Dr. Paige Miller) was Miss California.

In 1995, Farah Fath (Gigi Morasco) was crowned Miss Kentucky Preteen.

Both Kamar de Los Reyes (Antonio Vega) and Michael Easton (John McBain) have landed on *People* magazine's annual list of the 50 Most Beautiful People in the World.

Sports

Thorsten Kaye (Patrick Thornhart) traveled throughout Europe playing rugby.

Ty Treadway (Drs. Colin and Troy MacIver) was named 1994's Mr. Natural Pennsylvania, a bodybuilding competition.

Michael Storm (Dr. Larry Wolek) fenced competitively.

Larry Lau (Sam Rappaport) holds a black belt in karate, a skill that came in quite handy when a lunatic attacked him outside a restaurant in New York.

Jason-Shane Scott (Will Rappaport) managed to get onto his high school baseball team during his senior year despite the fact that he had never played before. And he even set a new school record, having been hit by the ball every time he was at bat.

Game Shows

Before Kassie DePaiva (Blair Cramer) began her soap opera career, she competed on the charades-themed game show *Body Language*. Her celebrity partner was Catherine Hickland (Lindsay Rappaport), who was working on *Capitol* at the time. DePaiva, who didn't win any serious money, walked away with the typical game show parting gifts: a can of cooking spray and an electric broom.

On the talent show *Star Search,* Joe Lando (Jake Harrison) was beaten in the acting category by Scott Thompson Baker, who himself went on to a lengthy career in daytime (*General Hospital, All My Children,* and *The Bold and the Beautiful*).

Bruce Michael Hall (Joey Buchanan) looked for love on two of MTV's dating game shows: *Singled Out* and *Dismissed.*

In the early nineties, Don Jeffcoat, who also played Joey Buchanan, hosted the Nickelodeon game show *Wild & Crazy Kids.*

Ty Treadway (Colin and Troy MacIver) currently hosts *Merv Griffin's Crosswords.*

Military Service

Phil Carey (Asa Buchanan) served in two wars, World War II and the Korean War. During World War II, Carey was traveling to Japan on a carrier that was bombed.

Jeremy Slate, who played Asa's right-hand man Chuck Wilson, also served in World War II. He joined the navy at the age of sixteen. By age eighteen, he was invading Omaha Beach on D-Day.

Robert S. Woods (Bo Buchanan) did not need to serve in Vietnam. As a college student, he had been given a deferment, but he opted to drop out to join the army. Because he'd suffered rheumatic fever as a child and always needed to take it easy, Woods was dying for a real physical challenge. Just to test himself, he signed on to join the Green Berets.

Nicholas Coster (Anthony Makana) is a licensed skipper with the U.S. Coast Guard.

David Fumero (Cristian Vega), who joined the marines straight out of high school and spent one year in active duty, fractured his ankle twice during boot camp.

Famous Relatives

Erika Slezak's (Victoria Lord Davidson) father, Walter Slezak, won the 1955 Tony Award for Best Actor in a Musical for his performance in *Fanny.* He was also well known for his work in films such as the Alfred Hitchcock classic *Lifeboat*. Erika Slezak's grandfather, Leo Slezak, was also famous as a world-renowned opera singer.

Paul Satterfield (Dr. Spencer Truman) comes from quite the musical family. His aunt is singer Rita Coolidge ("We're All Alone," "Higher and Higher") while his stepfather is Booker T., lead singer for Booker T. & the M.G.s.

Jeffrey Byron's (Richard Abbott) mother, Anna Lee, played Lila Quartermaine on *General Hospital* for over twenty years.

Arlene Dahl's (Lucinda Schenk) son Lorenzo Lamas starred on *Falcon Crest* in the 1980s and more recently on *The Bold and the Beautiful.*

Tonja Walker (Alex Olanov) is cousins with country singer Billy Ray Cyrus, whose wife, Leticia, loves the show. Walker is also a cousin once removed to Miley Cyrus, better known as Hannah Montana.

Nathan Fillion's (Joey Buchanan) ancestor Jubal Early fought in the Civil War as a lieutenant general for the Confederacy. When Nathan Fillion mentioned this to Joss Whedon, who created the sci-fi series *Firefly* on which Fillion starred, Whedon named a bounty hunter after Early.

Casper Van Dien's (Tyler Moody) great-great-great uncle was Mark Twain.

James DePaiva (Max Holden) is descended from Andrew Johnson, or as DePaiva likes to describe him, "the one who got impeached." (Mary Kay Adams, who as Death tried to claim Max, is descended from two presidents, John Adams and John Quincy Adams.)

The Names Have Been Changed

Mark Brettschneider (Jason Webb) was advised to change his name to something more marketable for the entertainment industry.[37] He refused. (He also ignored suggestions to undergo plastic surgery to remove the scar under his left eye.) Unlike Brettschneider, several cast members from *One Life to Live* have undergone name changes, both major and minor—and not always of their own choosing.

Phil Carey (Asa Buchanan) was born with the first name Eugene; Kale Browne (Sam Rappaport) with the first name David; and Anthony George (Dr. Will Vernon) with the first name Octavio.

Anthony, as it turned out made not only a good first name, but a good last name as well. So thought Gerald Anthony Buccarelli (Marco Dane), who lopped off his last name.

Like Anthony, Ilene Kristen (Roxy Balsom) also uses her middle name rather than her given last name, Schatz.

Kristen's on-screen son John-Paul Lavoisier (Rex Balsom)

first tested out his stage name in high school. A music teacher had warned Lavoisier that his given last name, Seponski, might hold him back in the entertainment business. Taking the teacher's advice to heart, Lavoisier decided to find something more dramatic. In biology class the next day, he happened upon the name Antoine-Laurent Lavoisier. (Eighteenth-century scientist Antoine-Laurent Lavoisier is considered the father of modern chemistry.) At first, John-Paul used Lavoisier on his research papers, and later he performed in the school talent show under that name. Some fans have wondered if the double first name might also have been his own creation, but that he got from his mother, who found the name John itself just too common.

When Bruce Michael Hall joined the actors' union, the name Bruce Hall was already taken. So was Bruce Robert Hall, his given name, and Bruce R. Hall. Not wanting to change his first name, he opted to change his middle. He chose Michael, which is his twin brother Seth's (*Passions*) middle name. Their whole lives they had shared everything else, he reasoned—why not their middle name?

Judith Light (Karen Wolek), born Licht, "light"-ened her name, changing the "c" to a "g."

Jacqueline Courtney (Pat Ashley) was born with the first name Sharon, but her parents changed it while she was still an infant.

Although Tuc Watkins's (David Vickers) parents named him Charles Curtis Watkins III, they tried to call him by his middle name. Watkins, who often spoke backward as a child, turned Curt into Tuc. His agent suggested that he add a "k" onto the name, but Watkins declined, preferring the spelling as it had been his whole life.

While some actors shorten their names, Thorsten Kaye shortened his all the way down to one letter, or to the phonetic spelling of that letter. Kaye had been born in Germany with the last name Kieselbach.

When Linda Dano (Gretel Rae Cummings) returned to *One Life to Live* in 1999, the character had dropped her first name in favor of her middle name, Rae. Dano, born Linda Wildermuth, had shortened her own name as well. Dano evolved from Giordano, the last name of her second husband. (Dano is not the only actress from the show to have truncated an ex-husband's last name. She wasn't even the only Linda to do so. Linda Thorson [Julia Medina] nee Robinson dropped the first syllable off her one-time married name of Bergthorson.)

Andrea Evans and Krista Tesreau, who both played Tina Lord, took their husbands' names after they got married. Andrea hyphenated Massey onto Evans while Tesreau became Krista Mione. After their respective divorces, both Tinas reverted back to their original names.

Several of the show's leading ladies have taken their husband's name even after having established their own, among them Kassie (Wesley) DePaiva (Blair Cramer), Laura (Bonariggo) Koffman (Cassie Callison), and Phylicia (Ayers-Allen) Rashad (Courtney Wright). Hillary B. Smith (Nora Hanen) went by Hillary Bailey when she was on *The Doctors* and Hillary Bailey Smith for a while after getting married, but has abbreviated her maiden name into a middle initial.

Even less common than seeing an actress take her husband's name is finding a man, famous or not, who will take his wife's name. Yet Wortham Krimmer (Andrew Carpenter) did just that. Born Robert Krimmer, he hyphenated his wife Maryellen's last name to his own, becoming Robert Wortham-Krimmer. When the name took up too much space on a theater program, he lopped off his first name. Although known professionally as Wortham Krimmer, he answers to Bob. After telling this story in almost every interview he's granted, he has grown tired of talking about the name change.

As the end credits rolled by one afternoon, *OLTL* viewers noticed that the role of Brad Vernon was being played by Steve Blizzard. Steve Fletcher, who played Brad, had changed his name because he lost a bet about being able to crawl across the floor on his stomach. The last name Blizzard was chosen in honor of the weather conditions during which the bet was made. Eventually, Fletcher resumed using his own name.

Shawn Batten, who played a Monica Lewinsky–inspired character on the short-lived NBC soap opera *Sunset Beach,* could not use her given name of Susan because the acting union already had a Susan Batten, *One Life's* Luna Moody. The two finally met at an awards show, where Shawn walked over to Susan and announced, "You have my name."

Proud Parents

When John-Paul Lavoisier landed the role of Rex Balsom, his parents had T-shirts printed up reading: Dad of Rex and Mom of Rex. Lavoisier's mother actually wears her shirt outside the house.

After Mary Gordon Murray took over the role of Becky Lee Abbott, her father would shut down his CPA office every afternoon from 2:00 until 3:00 so that he could watch the show. He not only encouraged his clients to watch, he printed up business cards reminding them to do so.

Andrea Evans's (Tina Lord) father could not watch the often intense love scenes between Tina and Mitch Laurence (Roscoe Born).

Melissa Gallo (Adriana Cramer) e-mails her parents and grandmother the dates when her character will be doing sex scenes, so that they don't tune in.

Renee Elise Goldsberry's (Evangeline Williamson) mother, a psychologist, would not only watch the show, she would analyze the character of Evangeline. Goldsberry's husband, a lawyer, offered input on her legal scenes.

Don Jeffcoat's (Joey Buchanan) father would occasionally call up Julie Madison, the casting director who hired Jeffcoat, to see how his son was doing on the show.

Love in the Afternoon (and Evening)

Producers acknowledge it as a workplace hazard. When two good-looking actors are paired up together in romantic scene after romantic scene, make-believe kisses will occasionally spark into a real-life romance. Those sparks tend to catch in the *One Life to Live* studios almost as often as a fire breaks out in Llanview—even when you factor in that arsonist who was running loose around town.

Kassie DePaiva (Blair Cramer) did not like James De-Paiva (Max Holden) the first time she met him. Kassie, who was starring on *Guiding Light* at the time, was performing at the Whaler Bar in New York City. After her set, she met up with a record executive, who was interested in signing her to his label. While she was talking to the executive, James came up to compliment her on one of her songs. Because of his cocky attitude, Kassie misinterpreted the compliment as sarcasm and wrote him off as a jerk. It wasn't until years later that she realized he had honestly been complimenting her.[38]

Although both Kassie and James were married to other people when she joined *One Life to Live,* they couldn't deny their attraction to each other. On-screen, Blair was desperately trying to reconnect with her ex-lover Max, who had found happiness with Luna Moody (Susan Batten). Kassie fared much better with James: After divorcing their respective spouses, the two of them married on May 31, 1996. They had each already experienced the big wedding: 450 guests attended Kassie's first wedding; the reception for James's first wedding to *Hee Haw* honey Misty Rowe was hosted by country superstar Kenny Rogers. For this wedding, James and Kassie opted for something far more private, just the two of them and a justice of the peace. They renewed their vows a couple of weeks later so that they could include James's daughter Dreama in the process.

Despite rumors to the contrary, the DePaivas never demanded that they work together; they never even requested it. Max and Blair were, however, eventually paired back together and got married. During the Max and Blair love scenes, James DePaiva would give his wife the same sort of stage kiss he gave all his leading ladies. Max and Blair's marriage was short-lived, unlike James and Kassie's, which has lasted now for twelve years and counting.

Thorsten Kaye's audition to play Patrick Thornhart required him to kiss future leading lady Susan Haskell (Marty Saybrooke). Before the audition, Haskell warned him not to slip his tongue into her mouth. That warning became fodder for teasing once the two actors fell in love off-screen as well as on. In 1996, when the two decided to leave the show together, Marty finally married her beloved

Patrick Thornhart (Thorsten Kaye) and Marty Saybrooke's (Susan Haskell) love story sparked an off-screen romance for Kaye and Haskell.

Patrick. In California, Haskell landed a recurring role on *JAG*, and Kaye joined *Port Charles* as Patrick's lookalike brother, Ian. During one story line, Haskell guested as the ghost of Ian's (and hence Patrick's) late sister Granya. *One Life to Live* viewers were more than a little disturbed to imagine that Patrick Thornhart had fallen in love with the spitting image of his dead sister. For that very reason, the producers had initially considered applying some sort of prosthetics to Haskell's face to disguise her appearance. When Kaye returned to the East Coast to work on *All My Children*, *One Life* fans were hoping that Haskell would be coming back to Llanview. (She had returned for a few episodes in 2002.) Unfortunately, the real-life romance between Kaye and Haskell prevented her resuming her role.

Because Haskell was pregnant with her and Kaye's second child, she could not step back into the character when it was being reintroduced.

Taking a cue from Bo Buchanan's romance with Mimi King, their portrayers, Robert S. Woods and Kristen Meadows, began dating. The romance was short-lived. As a result, so too was the romance between Bo and Mimi. When the writers noted the change in chemistry between the two actors, they quickly brought that story line to an end.[39] (Woods's real wife Loyita Chapel, whom he, in perfect soap opera fashion, married twice, has appeared on the show twice. In 1988, during the Wild West story line, she played Bo's great-great-great grandmother Blaize Buchanan. More recently, she popped up in Llanview as Dallas, his brother Clint's girlfriend.)

Gerald Anthony (Marco Dane) and Brynn Thayer (Jenny Wolek) might never have gotten together as a couple were it not for the game show *The $20,000 Pyramid*. Although their characters were very closely linked to Judith Light's Karen Wolek—Marco as her pimp, Jenny as her sister—Anthony and Thayer had not worked extensively together. To be honest, they "weren't nuts about each other at first."[40] The two of them were picked to represent *One Life to Live* during a soap opera tournament on *Pyramid*, pitting them against teams from the other ABC soaps. Determined to win, Anthony bought a version of the home game and brought it over to Thayer's apartment after work nights to practice. Spending so much time together, the two soon fell in love. They also won more than $20,000 for the Save the Children Foundation. The writers toyed with the idea of pairing Marco up with Jenny, but the characters didn't belong together as much as the actors did. Although the marriage lasted only a couple of years, Thayer credits Anthony with teaching her to stand up for herself.

Stephen Schnetzer (Marcello Salta) fell in love with Nancy Snyder (Katrina Karr) the first time he laid eyes on her in the studio. Their characters were involved briefly, but Marcello could not handle Katrina's past career as a prostitute. Schnetzer and Snyder married the same year that Schnetzer left *One Life* for *Another World*. Snyder retired from acting the following year to concentrate on raising a family. She did, however, work with her husband on *Another World* in a short-term role as his psychiatrist.

While Tina Clayton (Andrea Evans) never won country singer Johnny Drummond's (Wayne Massey) heart, Evans herself fared much better with Massey. In the fall of 1980, after the end of a workday, a hansom carriage was waiting for Massey and Evans, who had been dating for a while at this point. The carriage whisked them away to Central Park, where Massey popped the question. Between Tina's heavy story line and Massey's concert tour, the wedding needed to be rescheduled a couple of times, but the two finally tied the knot the following April. During their marriage, which lasted three years, Massey encouraged Evans to explore her singing potential and often called her up to sing with him onstage, including once at the Grand Ole Opry in Nashville.

In 1981, Karen Wolek (Judith Light) infiltrated a counterfeiting ring to discover who had killed her ex-brother-in-law Vinnie Wolek (Michael Ingram). Toward that end, she feigned a romantic interest in Steve Piermont (Robert Desiderio), a higher-up in the organization. Just as

Karen's charade led into real feelings for Steve, so too did Light's performance lead into real feelings for Desiderio. When Light decided to leave the show, Desiderio returned, allowing Karen and Steve to run away together. Light and Desiderio were married in a very private ceremony in Aspen, Colorado, on New Year's Day, 1985.

Fiona Hutchison (Gabrielle Medina) was taken with John Viscardi (Fr. Tony Vallone) the very first moment she saw him on the set. So taken that she became very self-conscious about the way she looked with her hair a mess and wearing old clothes.[41] Although Viscardi himself was dressed only in jeans and a shirt, Hutchison was amazed by how handsome he looked. Immediately, she raced back to her dressing room, where she showered, fixed her hair, and pulled on a nice dress. As the two got to know each other, looks and fashion became less important. Viscardi didn't even wear a shirt to their wedding. In an unconventional ceremony, the two married while hiking in the Grand Canyon. Hutchison herself opted for a Victoria's Secret teddy rather than a wedding dress—and she wore that with hiking boots, backpack, and a fedora to match Viscardi's.

Vanita Harbour (Rika Price) did not like Allan Dean Moore (Kerry Nichols) the first time that they met. Since he didn't know anyone else in New York, Harbour took pity and showed him around the city. She found him far too immature. He didn't care much for her either.[42] But working together as an on-screen couple, Harbour and Moore warmed up to each other and eventually fell in love. While show business had brought them together, their careers nearly broke them apart. After leaving *OLTL,* Moore stayed in New York while Harbour headed out to California to work on a play. The opening night of the play, with all of Harbour's family in attendance, Moore proposed, but a miniseries he was filming in the Caribbean nearly kept him from the wedding. The production schedule had been thrown off track, and the producer was not going to let him fly home. At the last minute, after much prodding, the producer finally relented. After a fifteen-hour flight, Moore arrived home just in time for his bachelor party. Dead tired, he could not stay awake during the reception. At four o'clock in the morning, he flew back down to the Carribean with Harbour. They combined the end of filming with their honeymoon.

Throughout Gina Tognoni's run as Kelly Cramer, the character was involved off and on with Joey Buchanan, played by Nathan Fillion and Don Jeffcoat, both of whom Tognoni herself dated. Tognoni also dated Joey's on-screen stepfather Mark Derwin (Ben Davidson). Although Kelly and Ben were never involved, on *Guiding Light,* Tognoni's character Dinah Marler recently married A. C. Mallett, a role originated by Derwin.

Following in the tradition of Fillion and Jeffcoat, Bruce Michael Hall (who played Joey in 2003) also dated his leading lady, Jessica Morris (Jen Rappaport, who married, then cheated on, Joey).

The romance between Antonio Vega (Kamar de los Reyes) and Keri Reynolds (Sherri Saum) ended badly, very badly. Distraught over her breakup with Antonio and his new relationship with Jessica Buchanan (Bree Williamson), Keri committed suicide. The romance, however, continued happily, very happily for Kamar de los Reyes and Sherri Saum. In May of 2007, De los Reyes and Saum were married in a bilingual ceremony, honoring his Puerto Rican heritage. Prior to De los Reyes, Saum had dated her *Sunset Beach* costar Timothy Adams, who occasionally pops up in Llanview as Marcie's brother Ron Walsh.

When De los Reyes's on-screen brother David Fumero (Cristian Vega) first asked out De los Reyes's on-screen sister Melissa Gallo (Adriana Cramer), she turned him down because he was too good-looking. Her experience with men up to that point, she told *Soap Opera Digest,* had trained her that the really good-looking ones tended to be arrogant and full of themselves. Fumero persisted, and the two eventually became a couple. At first, Fumero thought they should keep the relationship secret (he had learned his lesson during an on-again/off-again relationship with Erin Torpey [Jessica Buchanan]), but once he decided to leave the show in 2003, he no longer worried about who knew they were dating. On Valentine's Day, he sent Gallo an enormous bouquet of flowers at the studio. The two were married in November 2007.

Backstage romance does not brew merely between actors and actors. Anthony Call (Herb Callison) has been married for more than twenty years to Margo Husin, who is now the show's postproduction supervisor.

Call's onetime leading lady Louise Sorel (Judith Sanders) became involved with Paul Rauch, who was then executive producing the show. Looking back on the relationship, she considered it a mistake and cited it as one of the reasons why she left the show after only a year.[43]

It's a Thin Line of Dialogue
Between Love and Hate

Just as producers worry about their actors falling in love with each other, they also worry about their actors not getting along—especially if two of them are expected to play lovers. While some actors have worked through their animosities, other on-screen romances have been shelved because of the actors' noticeable dislike for each other.

Robert S. Woods (Bo Buchanan) and Jacqueline Courtney (Pat Ashley) were standing beside each other in a party scene when it occurred to the producers that the two of them looked good together. Thinking that Bo and Pat could become the show's next big couple, the producers even sent them off to Paris for a romantic location shoot. While they may have looked good standing next to each other, Woods and Courtney didn't get along exceptionally well. Off the set, they barely spoke to each other and never ran their lines together. Eventually the producers gave up trying to make Bo and Pat work as a couple and found each of the actors new love interests.

When asked about his most difficult day on the set, Clint Ritchie (Clint Buchanan) once told *Soap Opera Digest* that he considered any day he had to work with Barbara Luna (Maria Roberts) a very bad day. The character of Maria had been brought onto the show as a potential spoiler in Clint's marriage to Viki. Maria had not only been Clint's first girlfriend, she had borne him a son. Ritchie's reluctance to work with Luna, especially to do love scenes with her, KO'd that story line. Maria concentrated her efforts on breaking up her son Cord's (John Loprieno) marriage to Tina Lord (Andrea Evans). Unlike Ritchie, both Loprieno and Evans loved working with Luna.

From the audition, Ellen Holly (Carla Hall) could not stand Arthur Burghardt (Dr. Jack Scott). While Dr. Scott was supposed to treat Carla with contempt in their first meeting, Holly could tell that the condescension coming from Burghardt was legitimate. As a theater actor, Burghardt considered the entire medium beneath him. Holly begged producer Joe Stuart not to hire the man; when Stuart did, she broke down in tears. Beyond Burghardt's condescension, she found his professionalism lacking. He would often arrive late to the set without knowing his lines. Trying to make the best of a bad situation, Holly offered to run lines with him, an offer he declined with an insulting comment about how she took soap operas too seriously. Adding to her woes, she was accused by the producer of trying to intimidate the newcomer.[44]

Anthony Call (Herb Callison) and Robin Strasser (Dorian Lord) came to *One Life to Live* as veteran performers. Call had worked on both The *Edge of Night* and *Guiding Light,* Strasser on *Another World* and *All My Children.* While

Strasser and Call were both dedicated and highly talented, their styles often clashed—as did Strasser and Call. After one particularly heated on-set argument, both actors retreated to their respective dressing rooms. A little while later, Strasser slipped a note under Call's door: "Tony," the note read, "we have a chance to do something really great here. And the line at unemployment is very long." Realizing that Strasser was right, Call resolved to work out their differences.

Although their characters hit it off almost immediately, Joe Lando (Jake Harrison) and Jessica Tuck (Megan Gordon) took a little more time warming up to each other. He

Although Megan Gordon (Jessica Tuck) and Jake Harrison (Joe Lando) fell in love almost immediately, Tuck and Lando took a little longer warming up to each other.

and Tuck disliked each other so intensely that Lando wanted to quit his very first week. During "Where Are They Now?" interviews with *Soap Opera Digest,* Lando laughs at how he cannot even remember what he and Tuck used to fight about. The tension reached its peak during the mystery surrounding Michael Grande's (Dennis Parlato) murder, where both Jake and Megan were considered suspects. Brian Tarantina, who played Jake's best friend Lucky Lippman, was friends with both Lando and Tuck; he asked the two of them to meet him at a local bar after work. Neither knew that the other had been invited. Once they arrived, Tarantina excused himself and strongly suggested to them that they work out their differences over a couple of drinks. By the end of the night, Lando and Tuck considered themselves friends.

Two Women for Every Man

While Nora Hanen and Lindsay Rappaport have not been feuding for quite as long as Viki Lord Davidson and Dorian Lord, Nora and Lindsay have packed a lot of hatred and resentment into the ten years they've known each other. As with Viki (who happens to be one of Nora's best friends) and Dorian (one of Lindsay's closest allies), the Nora/Lindsay feud involves countless insults, infinite scheming, short-lived truces, a little kidnapping, the occasional murder, and a string of men to fight over . . .

Sam Rappaport

The man who started all the trouble between Lindsay and Nora. Lawyer Sam Rappaport married Lindsay but always carried a torch for Nora, whom he had known in college. Sam's reignited feelings for his college sweetheart undermined Lindsay's attempts to reconcile with her ex-husband. Lindsay, it should be mentioned, would eventually kill Sam—by accident; she thought she was shooting at Troy MacIver, another one of the men she and Nora would come to share.

Bo Buchanan

Blaming Nora for the trouble between Sam and herself, Lindsay decided to wreak a little havoc in Nora's life. She altered the results of Bo's sperm count test. When Nora discovered that she was pregnant, she—and Bo—believed that the father was Sam Rappaport, with whom Nora had cheated in order to get pregnant. As soon as Bo and Nora split, Lindsay worked her way into Bo's life and wound up both engaged to Bo and expecting his child. When Nora revealed that Lindsay had changed Bo's sperm test, Bo dumped Lindsay, and she lost the baby. For both those devastations, she blamed Nora and plotted to take everything away from her. With the help of her ex-brother-in-law, Dr. Colin MacIver, Lindsay injected Nora with a drug that erased her memory.

Troy MacIver

Colin's twin brother, Troy, also a doctor, came to town and fell in love with Nora. To prove his love, he tricked Lindsay into confessing on tape what she had done to Nora's memory. Lindsay briefly went to prison and came out looking for revenge against Troy and Nora, who were now a couple. Lindsay dug up dirt about Troy's role in the death of his late wife. (The woman killed herself after a fight between them.) With that information, Lindsay blackmailed Troy into an affair. Nora caught the two of them in bed together, and Troy realized it wasn't the best game plan, sleeping with Lindsay to keep her from revealing information that *might* ruin his relationship with Nora. Lindsay might have felt satisfied with her revenge had she not fallen in love with yet another man hung up on Nora.

Daniel Colson

Lindsay dated lawyer Daniel Colson but found herself more attracted to a younger man, Rex Balsom. Daniel simply moved on to colleague Nora Hanen, whom he married, although, like Lindsay, he too preferred the company of younger men.

RJ Gannon

While grieving over the murder of her daughter Jen (who was murdered by her ex Daniel Colson), Lindsay turned to RJ Gannon, Nora's ex-brother-in-law, with whom Nora shared a brief sexual history. Lindsay resented the fondness RJ still felt for Nora, but a triangle never developed.

Clint Buchanan

While Nora's ex Bo Buchanan has rediscovered his feelings for Lindsay, Nora is developing feelings for Bo's brother Clint, who also happens to be Lindsay's ex-husband.

5
The Plot Thickens

Christening Day

After a parrot flew into Todd Manning's penthouse and stuck around, the show allowed the viewers a chance to name it. The unlikely name Moose was chosen. For the most part, the writers don't leave naming the human characters in the hands of the fans.

Agnes Nixon christened the aristocratic Lords after the family in the Philip Barry play *The Philadelphia Story*, which was made into the 1940 Katharine Hepburn/Cary Grant/Jimmy Stewart film of the same name. Victoria Lord spells her nickname Viki to reflect the family's Germanic roots.

Viki Lord's alternate personality was given the name Niki Smith (a) because Niki rhymed with Viki, and (b) because of the contrast between Lord and Smith, Lord being a royal title and Smith (derived from blacksmith) representing the working class, with whom Niki hung around.

The character of Sadie Gray was named after Agnes Nixon's own longtime housekeeper, Sadie Gray. Although named after a real person, the family name Gray provided an apt charactonym for Sadie's daughter Carla (Ellen Holly), a light-skinned black woman trying to pass as white.

Clint Ritchie objected to his character's proposed name, Chris Logan. To Ritchie, a cowboy at heart, the name didn't sound like someone who could ride a horse. If Ritchie wanted the character to have a cowboy name, the writers were happy to oblige, naming the character Clint after Ritchie himself.[45] In turn, Ritchie was eventually nicknamed after his character. Phil Carey, who played Clint's father, Asa, took to calling Ritchie Bucky, short for Buchanan.

Bo, as in Clint's brother Bo Buchanan, is a shortened form of his full name, Beaufort Oglethorpe. Robert S. Woods, who plays Bo, told *Soap Opera Digest* that he hated Ralston, the last name Bo went by when he believed that ranch hand Yancey Ralston was his biological father.

Asa Buchanan's middle name—actually middle names plural and occasional alias—is Jeb Stuart, a former cavalry officer and Robert E. Lee's onetime aide-de-camp during the Civil War. Asa's name could grow even longer when you take into consideration that Jeb was short for James Ewell Brown.

The name Reverend Andrew Carpenter was chosen as a deliberate reference to Jesus Christ, who was a carpenter and who counted Andrew among his apostles.

When the writers brought Mitch Laurence back from the grave in 2002, he was going by the name Michael Lazarus, a none too subtle biblical reference to his resurrection.

Nora Hanen showed up as the ex-wife of D.A. Hank Gannon and fell into a romance with Bo Buchanan. Picking up on the Gannon/Buchanan rhyme, the writers also revealed before her wedding to Bo that her maiden name had been Hanen, making her full name then Nora Hanen Gannon Buchanan.

Marty Saybrooke's last name was chosen to represent old money, taken from the town of Old Saybrook, Connecticut. Although the character was christened Margaret, she went by the male nickname Marty to show her rebellious side.

The fact that Todd Manning was forced into sex (in essence raped) by a woman named Margaret (Cochran), the same given name as his own rape victim Marty, was not lost on viewers for its sense of poetic justice.

Jake Harrison was originally going to be named Ross, until the producers realized that there were a few too many Rosses already on daytime (including Jerry ver Dorn's character, Ross Marler, on *Guiding Light*).

After playing Felicia Gallant on *Another World* for almost two decades, Linda Dano was not looking forward to playing a character with the far less glamorous name of Gretel that she had originated in the 1970s. She and the producers decided that Gretel could now be going by a middle name and picked Rae, which was Dano's own middle name. The on-screen story behind Gretel's name change came out later when it was revealed that Rae had been practicing psychology under the credentials of a Ray Cummings, a man.

BethAnn Bonner's character was originally going to be named Rhonda. Since the police detective she was playing was being introduced during the arson/white supremacist story line, the producers thought it would give the character and the story more depth for the role to be made ethnic, so she was renamed Talia Sahid and the character given an Arab-American heritage.

Few characters if any aside from River Carpenter can lay

claim to being named in honor of a suicide attempt. River's biological mother Beth Garvey (Dorothy Barton) once planned on killing herself by jumping into Llanview River. In honor of her decision not to jump, she named her son River. (Matthew Twining, who played River as a teenager, often introduced himself to reporters as River Carpenter.)

The unluckiest name for children in Llanview seems to be Megan. Joe Riley's affair with Cathy Craig in the mid-seventies produced a baby girl name Megan, who died as an infant. The name was used again in the late eighties when Viki discovered a long-lost daughter, Megan Gordon. Three years later, Megan contracted lupus and died. Megan's sister Jessica decided to honor her by naming her own daughter Megan. That baby died shortly after its premature birth, a birth brought on when Jessica was run down by Dorian Lord.

Jessica probably wouldn't have named her second daughter Brennan after the baby's father, Nash Brennan, if she had anticipated that she would end up marrying Nash, thereby straddling the child with the repetitive name Brennan Brennan. Then again, Brennan would be growing up in a town where the late assistant district attorney was named Hugh Hughes.

They Grow Up So Fast

Soap operas usually send children away to summer camp or boarding school to bring them back older. Defying such convention, Starr Manning literally aged two years in a matter of three months right before the audience's very eyes. In December of 2003, Starr mentioned to her father that she was nine years old. In January, a line of dialogue referred to her as ten. By February, she was eleven.

When Erin Torpey grew literally eight inches in less than a year, the producers decided to age the character of Jessica two years, placing her at Torpey's real-life age.

In 1988, Michael Storm discovered that soap opera rapid age syndrome was not restricted to children. After decades playing Larry Wolek as younger than Viki, Storm discovered that Larry was now several years older than she. To suit the needs of a history rewrite that found a teenaged Viki giving birth to a daughter, the writers reinvented Larry's own backstory, placing him in medical school and capable of delivering a baby while Viki was still in high school.

Crossing the Line

In the past decade, ABC has launched two major crossover story lines for its soaps: Rae Cummings searched through Llanview, Pine Valley, and Port Charles for her long-lost daughter. Several years after Rae reunited with her daughter, *All My Children*'s Little Adam Chandler was taken away from his mother Babe (Alexa Havins) and given to *OLTL*'s Kelly Cramer (Heather Tom). While never done on quite this scale, crossovers are not new to ABC. They date all the way back to *One Life to Live*'s first year on the air.

Steve Hardy (John Beradino) from *OLTL*'s lead-in, *General Hospital,* paid a visit to Llanview Hospital to consult on Meredith Lord's (Trish Van Devere) case and to bring some of the *GH* audience in to check out the new soap. Larry Wolek (Michael Storm) did likewise when *All My Children* debuted in 1970, traveling from Llanview to Pine Valley Hospital.

If you can imagine a time when a rich woman couldn't find a suitable lawyer in Llanview, Viki Lord Davidson

Rae Cummings (Linda Dano, right) traveled to Pine Valley (*All My Children*), Port Charles (*General Hospital*, *Port Charles*) and back to Llanview in search of her long-lost daughter. Also pictured: Viki Lord Davidson (Erika Slezak, left).

hired Pine Valley's Paul Martin (William Mooney) to defend her when she was accused of murdering Marco Dane.

On his way from Pine Valley to Corinth (setting for the now defunct *Loving*), Jeremy Hunter (Jean LeClerc) stopped off in Llanview long enough to rescue artwork from a burning Llanfair.

Back when Dorian Lord (then Elaine Princi) was publishing the *National Intruder*, her old friend *All My Children*'s Adam Chandler (David Canary) would plant nasty stories about his enemies in the paper. Dorian returned the favor years later by giving Adam dirt on her nephew's not-so-ex-wife Babe, who had married Adam's son.

Liza Colby (Marcy Walker) from *All My Children* hired Nora Hanen to represent her in a sexual harassment case.

All My Children's Tad Martin (Michael E. Knight) showed up on *One Life to Live* when Nora Hanen and her family appeared on his talk show *The Cutting Edge* to air out all their family's dirty secrets. (Knight returned to the show for a special Valentine's Day episode where he appeared as a mysterious stranger in the fantasy of Lindsay Rappaport, played by Knight's then wife Catherine Hickland.)

Robin Christopher had been in discussions with *All My Children* to reprise the role of Skye Chandler, when the idea was presented to introduce the character on *One Life to Live* as Ben Davidson's ex-wife. From there, Christopher moved Skye to Port Charles and *General Hospital*, which tapes on the West Coast, where she wanted to live. Although Skye initially moved to Port Charles to know her biological father, Alan Quartermaine, the writers at *GH* undid the fact that Alan was her father.

After years of wreaking havoc and running scams in Llanview, Marco Dane popped up in Port Charles, where he aided Tracy Quartermaine in her varied schemes. *General Hospital* earned Gerald Anthony an Emmy for his work as Marco.

While Thorsten Kaye did not bring Patrick Thornhart to *Port Charles,* he did play Patrick's lookalike brother, Ian, using their shared back history.

Some crossovers just never happened . . .

After Kamar de los Reyes left New York for the West

Coast, ABC toyed with the idea of transferring Antonio Vega onto *Port Charles,* adding him to the PCPD.

Joe Lando wanted to bring Jake Harrison and his buddy Lucky Lippman onto *General Hospital.*

For years, Robert S. Woods has dreamed of a crossover romance, even a short-term fling, between Bo Buchanan and *All My Children*'s Erica Kane.[46]

What They Meant to Write

An actor leaves a show, an actor or character become far more popular than expected, a couple becomes too popular to break up, a story line proves just too controversial—for any number of reasons, story lines have been abandoned and/or rerouted halfway through.

The character of Asa Buchanan had originally been brought on for a year. He was supposed to either die from a heart attack or be murdered. Asa did die of a heart attack—just twenty-seven years behind schedule.

The recently widowed Pat Ashley was intended to be part of a love triangle with longtime nemesis Dorian Lord and Dorian's ex-flame David Renaldi, who had recently been introduced on the show. Unfortunately, this plot development came after actress Jacqueline Courtney had been lingering around the show for too long without a story line and had already made plans to leave. Instead, Jenny Janssen took over Pat's place in the triangle.

At one point, the character of Sadie Gray considered giving up her position as head of housekeeping at Llanview

Hospital to work as a maid in the Siegel household. Lillian Hayman and her on-screen daughter Ellen Holly (Carla Gray) convinced the producers that Sadie, one of the only two black women on the show, giving up the position she had to become a maid in a white family's home would send out a terrible message.[47]

The writers brought back the character of Viki's cousin Richard Abbott in the mid-eighties as part of a love triangle with Tina Lord and Cord Roberts. When it became apparent that Tina and Cord were evolving into a supercouple, Richard felt extraneous. The writers then planned to pair him up with Cassie Callison (Ava Haddad) in a sophisticated love story. Haddad's plans to leave the show killed that idea.

During the summer of 1985, Paul Rauch tried to capitalize on the popularity of the *Friday the 13th*–style of movies by placing a number of the teen cast members in a lonely cabin in the woods, where mad scientist Ivan Kipling was hiding out. Ivan Kipling would then spend the summer terrorizing them. Rauch was so put off by the rehearsal scenes with the teens that he disbanded the story line altogether.

Angela Holliday (Susan Diol) was introduced as a con artist posing as an evangelist. While Angela was introduced to stir up trouble between Cain Rogan (Christopher Cousins) and his fiancée Tina Lord (Karen Witter), she was intended to then move on to causing trouble between Max Holden and Luna Moody. Angela would be enabling Max's gambling addiction. Upon closer examination, the writers decided that making Blair Cramer, with whom Max had a past history, the enabler would add another layer to the story.

Initially, the writers planned for Will Rappaport to be a virgin, for his first time with Jessica Buchanan (Erin Torpey) to be both of their first times. When the incredibly handsome Jason-Shane Scott was cast in the role, Will being a virgin no longer seemed quite as plausible.

Many viewers and Roger Howarth himself objected to the writers turning Todd Manning into a hero. More than likely, those same viewers would have revolted at the proposed story line that found Todd and Marty Saybrooke, the woman he raped, falling in love with each other.

When the character of RJ Gannon (Timothy D. Stickney) was at his most villainous, the plan was to have him killed off by his niece Rachel (Ellen Bethea, Mari Morrow, and Sandra P. Grant). To protect Rachel, her mother, Nora, would have confessed to the crime.

Nora, by the way, was originally intended to have been behind the wheel of the car that hit and killed Sarah Gordon (Grace Phillips). Nora would not have been legally responsible for the death because she was suffering from a brain tumor that caused blackouts. Nora's role in Sarah's death was to have been the obstacle for her relationship with Sarah's widower, Bo Buchanan. Robert S. Woods, who played Bo, couldn't imagine Bo staying in love with Nora burdened with that sort of baggage.[48] For the sake of the Bo/Nora romance, which had become an audience favorite, the story line was rewritten, blaming the accident on another driver.

In 1999, Linda Dano returned to *One Life to Live* as Gretel Cummings, now named Rae. The producers originally wanted her to play romance novelist Felicia Gallant, the *Another World* role that had won her a Best Actress

Emmy. Although *Another World* had been canceled, Procter & Gamble, which owned the rights to the character, would not sell them. P&G, which had transplanted a couple of characters from *Another World* onto *As the World Turns*, wanted to leave the door open for bringing Felicia onto *ATWT* or its other soap, *Guiding Light.*

If They Had a Choice

During the gang rape trial, Hillary B. Smith (Nora Hanen) was more than a little disturbed by the plot twist that her character would get Todd Manning and his cohorts exonerated of all charges. Given the powerful and dramatic telling of the story up to that point, Smith was worried about the message a not guilty verdict would send out[49]—so worried that she sat down with then executive producer Linda Gottlieb. Playing a lawyer must have rubbed off on Smith, who successfully argued her case. The story line was rewritten. Figuring out that Todd and crew were guilty, Nora all but admitted as much during the closing argument, forcing a mistrial. When more evidence surfaced before the next trial could begin, Todd and his fellow rapists entered plea bargains and were sent to prison.

Few actors have gotten their story lines changed as Smith did, but from time to time, actors do object to the material they have been given to play.

Between the numerous different personalities and the travels up to Heaven, underground to the city of Eterna, and back in time to the Old West, the writers have given Erika Slezak more than her fair share of outlandish story lines. As an actress, she maintains that it is her job to make the story line work, no matter what. That said, she absolutely hated the one in which Viki was being hypnotized into killing her son Kevin (then Kevin Stapleton). Even with the hypnosis excuse, she could not reconcile herself to Viki's actions.[50] Slezak did not refuse to play the story line, but she hated coming into work every day it was being taped.

After his wife Sarah died for a second time, a despondent Bo Buchanan climbed out on the ledge of a building, intending to jump. Robert S. Woods himself hated to see Bo even contemplating suicide.[51] Although he played the scene, he refused to turn Bo into a quivering ball of tears.

Before she left the show, Erin Torpey confessed to *Soap Opera Digest* that she was very disturbed by the plot twist that Jessica Buchanan was not Clint's biological daughter. Viewers and even Jessica's mother Viki discovered that Jessica's father was the villainous Mitch Laurence, who had raped her mother, a memory Viki had long repressed. According to *Soap Opera Digest*, even Clint Ritchie, who had not been on the show in years, resented the twist, as he had literally watched Torpey grow up playing his daughter.

Ritchie also disliked Clint's role in the homophobia story line. As a longtime journalist, Clint, he felt, should have been open-minded enough to accept not only Billy Douglas's homosexuality but Joey's friendship with Billy. Instead, a suddenly homophobic Clint was forbidding Joey from even speaking with his friend. Ritchie believes that the writers were intentionally making Clint less likable to make Viki look more sympathetic when she left him for Sloan

174 THE *ONE LIFE TO LIVE* 40TH ANNIVERSARY TRIVIA BOOK

Carpenter.[52] The audience shared Ritchie's dislike for Clint's homophobic attitude. For the first time since joining the show, Ritchie received negative fan mail.

Mark Dobies (Daniel Colson) told *Soap Opera Digest* that he did not have any problems with the revelation that his character was secretly sleeping with other men. What Dobies did have problems with: the fact that Daniel was killing people to keep his secret. In his mind, Dobies simply could not justify those murders.

While Roxy Balsom loves her doughnuts, Ilene Kristen, who tries to maintain a far healthier diet, cannot stand eating them during her scenes.

Although he didn't object to playing it, Kamar de los Reyes (who had by this point played out many scenes in various stages of undress) was embarrassed by the story line where Antonio went undercover as a male stripper.[53]

In on the Joke

During the weeks leading up to *One Life to Live*'s historic 10,000th episode, the writers inserted the number 10,000 into a line of dialogue every day. The soap opera, which can be among the funniest on daytime, has included a number of such inside jokes through the years.

One Life's soap-within-a-soap, *Fraternity Row*, satirized the soap opera community itself but never more pointedly than at the Daisy Awards, an awards ceremony *One Life* scheduled for June 29, opposite the 1989 Daytime Emmy Awards—a direct response, some figured, to the fact that *One Life to Live* had been nominated for only one Daytime Emmy that year (in the directing category). The *One Life* writers spoofed the titles of other soaps, like the 1988 Outstanding Drama Series winner *Santa Barbara,* which became *Santa Catalina;* the alliterative *The Bold and the Beautiful* became *The Wild and the Wealthy;* and *Days of Our Lives* became *The Day After Tomorrow.*

The Daisy Awards poked fun not only at the Daytime Emmys but at the *Soap Opera Digest* Awards, where *One*

The Daisy Awards gave *One Life to Live* the chance to spoof the Daytime Emmys. Soap actress Megan Gordon (Jessica Tuck) won a Daisy for Best Actress.

Life to Live had all too often been overlooked in favor of a *Days* landslide. At the Daisy Awards, *Fraternity Row* pulled a *Days* and swept every category in which it was nominated.

The ceremony even took a good-natured poke at *One Life to Live*'s own leading lady Erika Slezak. By this point, Slezak had already won two Best Actress awards, one of them for her riveting portrayal of Viki and her alternate personality Niki Smith. Viki's daughter and *Fraternity Row* star Megan Gordon had done her own alternate personality story line, which she believed guaranteed her the Best Actress Daisy—and she was right.

During the week in May 2002 when the show was

broadcast live, viewers spotted former cast members such as Jessica Tuck (Megan Gordon), Dennis Parlato (Michael Grande), and Susan Batten (Luna Moody) in the background. Tuck could actually be heard as well, gossiping about the Llanviewites around her. These actors then held up that day's end credits on cue cards. After a day or two, viewers realized that the show was not just bringing back any former cast members, but specifically those whose characters had been killed off. In essence, the show was bringing back dead characters for its live shows. By the end of the week, viewers were consciously looking for the cameo. Come the end of the Friday episode, they were wondering if they had missed someone, maybe someone from the distant past they wouldn't recognize. The show played one final joke during the end credits when Ty Treadway, who was holding up the cue cards, ripped open his shirt and revealed his chest, across which had been written that he was not Troy MacIver, but rather Troy's dead twin, Colin.

For Asa's second funeral, which was played for laughs since the character was not dead, the producers gathered together seven of the actresses who had played his wives through the years. The funeral was interspliced with clips from Asa's various weddings, including his 1992 union to Blair Cramer (then played by Asian-American actress Mia Korf). The flashback then cut back to Blair in church, now played by Kassie Depaiva, who immediately pulled out a small mirror to double-check her face.

Occasionally, an inside joke originates with the actor. In 1974, Erika Slezak's (Victoria Lord Riley) real-life father, character actor Walter Slezak, guested on the show as Viki's godfather Laszlo Braedeker. Walter Slezak took a line about

Viki being as beautiful as he remembered her and changed it. "Victoria," he said, "you are so beautiful, you could be my own daughter."

Years later, Viki was watching the Cary Grant movie *People Will Talk* with David Vickers. After the movie ended, she noted that as much as she always enjoyed Cary Grant, the actor playing his best friend stole the movie. Although she does not mention the actor by name, Slezak is talking about her real-life father, Walter.

Back in the late 1970s, as *General Hospital* was climbing in the ratings, it turned out that even the residents in Llanview were tuning in. The show came back from one commercial break to find the nurse outside Larry Wolek's office watching her portable TV. The audience could hear the trademark siren wail and theme music to *GH*'s opening credits. The nurse then picked up the phone to call another nurse and chat about the show.

In the early 1980s, the *One Life* cast included three alumni from *Dark Shadows*: Anthony George had been playing Dr. Will Vernon since the late seventies; Grayson Hall had recently joined the show as Southern matriarch Euphemia Ralston; and Nancy Barrett was recurring as District Attorney Debra Van Druten. Head writer Sam Hall, who had also written for *Dark Shadows,* paid homage to his former soap, placing Will, Euphemia, and Debra in a scene together even though their story lines were not intersecting. Looking at one another, all three remarked that the other two looked familiar but they could not place where they might know one another from.

During the early stage of their romance, Suede Pruitt (David Ledingham) took Marty Saybrooke out dancing, dirty dancing. Among the songs they danced to was "Do You Love Me" by The Contours, which had been featured in the film *Dirty Dancing,* a movie not coincidentally produced by *One Life to Live*'s then executive producer Linda Gottlieb.

When Marcie Walsh wrote *The Killing Club,* she credited a Professor Malone with helping her. Professor Malone was actually Michael Malone, the onetime *One Life to Live* head writer, who in real life did more than help; he had actually penned the novel. It was not the first time the show had referenced Michael Malone's other career, as a novelist. RJ Gannon was once spotted at his bar reading Malone's Christmas novel *The Last Noel.*

Sometimes, the inside joke is a sight gag, easily missed. On the bulletin board in Commissioner Buchanan's office, Robert S. Woods pinned up an article from *Soap Opera Digest* praising the Llanview police department.

Shortly after Matthew Ashford's character Jack Deveraux was slain by a psychiatrist/serial killer on *Days of Our Lives, One Life to Live* hired him to play a serial killer/psychology professor, Dr. Stephen Haver. During the murder investigation, John McBain (Michael Easton) questioned Dr. Haver's mother, Marlena (Patti Perkins)—who shared the same first name as the serial killer who had presumably done Jack in.

When Linda Dano (Rae Cummings) came back to *One Life to Live* in 1999 after the cancellation of *Another World,* where she'd been working since the mid-eighties, her character ran into several *AW* transplants. Rae's car was pulled over by John Sykes (John Bolger, who had played a police commissioner on *AW*). John told Rae that she looked familiar, then demanded a drunk driving test—a nod to Dano's Emmy-winning alcoholism story. In the police station, Rae asked Sam Rappaport (played by another *AW* alumnus, Kale Browne) to represent her.

During one of the many times that Evangeline Williamson (Renee Elise Goldsberry) was hospitalized, her sister Layla (Tika Sumpter) brought in a stuffed animal from home, a little Nala from *The Lion King*—a nice nod to Goldsberry's Broadway history. During Evangeline's first weeks in Llanview, Goldsberry had also been playing the role of Nala in the Broadway production of *The Lion King*.

In 1998, the show poked a little fun at its own history. Eleven years after sending the saintly Viki up to Heaven, the writers sent the less than saintly Dorian to Hell.

During one of of his classic action adventures, Bo Buchanan was crawling through the air vents in the Palace Hotel with Patrick Thornhart. When Patrick made a comment about sweating, Bo responded, "Never let them see you sweat," which had been the tagline from a long-running antiperspirant commercial actor Robert S. Woods made back in the eighties.

6
All for the Fans

Memorable Encounters with the Fans

y this point, actors who sign on to a soap opera understand how devoted fans become to their favorite shows. While *OLTL* actors grow accustomed to the crowds outside the ABC studios waiting for autographs, the actors are sometimes caught off guard by reminders of who exactly is watching.

Given the fact that Todd had led a gang rape against Marty Saybrooke and later killed her boyfriend Suede, Roger Howarth, who had a young son of his own, was horrified when a woman came up to tell him how much her seven-year-old liked him on the show.[54]

In the early 1980s, while Herb Callison (Tony Call) was married to Dorian, Call was stopped by the police late one night as he was walking home from a party. After frisking him, the officer asked Call, "Does Dorian know you're out this late?"

Thom Christopher (Carlo Hesser) was heading into the subway when a New York City police officer stopped him. Although Christopher plays one of daytime's more nefarious villains, he considers himself a law-abiding citizen. He couldn't imagine what business the police would have with him until the officer asked for an update on the prison riot story line.

Ken Meeker (Rafe Garretson) volunteered more than a few nights at homeless shelters around New York City. Many of those nights, he would not only prepare and serve dinner but sleep over in case any problems arose. He was more than a little surprised to discover that many of the homeless men he met managed to keep up with his story lines.

For years, Richard Merrell played Viki's butler Herron, a role he did not really expect people to remember. One night, while out to dinner with his good friend, renowned stage and screen actor Rex Harrison (*My Fair Lady*, *Doctor Dolittle*), Merrell was shocked when an autograph collector approached the table, asking him for his signature and paying absolutely no attention to Harrison.

Andrea Evans (Tina Clayton Lord) has always been recognizable by her long red hair. Back when she was first working on *One Life to Live,* some teenaged girls who spotted her asked if they could take a picture with her. While she was posing with a couple of the girls, one of their friends came up behind Evans with a pair of scissors and chopped off a sizable tress of her hair. The stylists on the set needed to layer Evans's hair so that the change would not be noticed.

Jessica Tuck (Megan Gordon) was surprised to find a crowd gathered around her apartment building when she was coming home from the studio one evening. She wondered if there had been a break-in or a fire until she got close enough to hear someone speaking in the manner of a tour guide: "And here," he was announcing, "is the home of *One Life to Live* actress Jessica Tuck." On her way into the building, Tuck removed her name from the buzzer.

Fans behind the counter at Krispy Kreme were all too happy to give Roscoe Born (Mitch Laurence) free doughnuts whenever he came in.

Few actors on the show have benefited from their celebrity more than Marilyn Chris (Wanda Wolek). Chris had been meeting with her agent, whose office was located in a somewhat dangerous building downtown. Coming out of the stall in the ladies' room, she was confronted by a couple of teenaged girls, one of whom was holding a knife. The girls demanded Chris's money. Nervous, Chris slipped into her soap opera persona, and one of the girls, a fan of the show, suddenly recognized Chris as Wanda. Rather than rob "Wanda," the two would-be muggers escorted Chris safely out of the building.

Fan Mail Call

For fans who cannot get themselves to New York to wait outside the ABC studios, the classic fan letter remains their best means of contacting their favorites.

Back in the 1970s, one faithful follower would send almost weekly letters to Ernest Graves when he was playing the role of Victor Lord. As soon as Victor lapsed into a coma, believing that Graves himself could no longer read his mail, the fan began writing to Victor's on-screen daughter Erika Slezak (Victoria Lord Riley), advising her how to care for her father.

One fan didn't appreciate Brynn Thayer's interpretation of Sister Jenny Wolek when she took over for Katherine Glass. The woman's letter suggested that Thayer give up acting and head back to the convent.

Whenever Lieutenant Ed Hall was investigating a crime, his portrayer, Al Freeman, Jr., would receive letters cluing him in on who really committed it.

An ardent group of Roy Thinnes (Sloan Carpenter) fans were determined to see that Viki leave her husband Clint for Sloan. Toward that end, the group not only started a letter-writing campaign, the members were writing up to ten letters apiece, signing each one with a different name.

During the story line in which Billy Douglas came out, Ryan Phillippe averaged a hundred letters a week from gay teenagers who were worried about coming out or were dealing with the ramifications of having come out. The producers hired a psychiatrist to help Phillippe provide answers to the fans who were writing to him.

During the height of the Todd Manning phenomenon, one of the secretaries at ABC would sort the fan mail into two large bags: one for Roger Howarth, the other for the rest of the cast.

Famous Fans

One of the first celebrities to admit being a soap opera fan was Lena Horne, who was drawn to *One Life* in part because of its strong African-American story line with Carla Gray and Ed Hall. While one of the first, Horne is far from the only celebrity fan who has tuned in to the show.

Promoting the big-screen soap spoof *Soapdish*, two-time Oscar winner Sally Field (*Norma Rae*, *Places in the Heart*) admitted that she herself watched soaps, among them *One Life to Live*.

Liza Minnelli was thrilled to meet "Cord Roberts" when John Loprieno went backstage after one of her performances.

Chandra Wilson from *Grey's Anatomy* lived out a fantasy at the 2007 Daytime Emmy Awards, where she met stars from all her favorite soaps, including *OLTL*, while hosting the red carpet preview show on SOAPnet.

In his best seller *Me Talk Pretty One Day*, humorist David Sedaris, whose pieces have appeared in *The New Yorker*, discussed how he used *One Life to Live* episodes to teach students how to write. In his autobiographical essay "Santa-Land Diaries," which was adapted into a stage play, Sedaris revealed a lifelong desire to be cast on the show. Despite that desire, he has turned down speaking roles, afraid that he'd be too nervous.[55] He has, however, earned a place of honor backstage. A wardrobe room at the studio has been named the David Sedaris Annex.

Kevin Williamson, who wrote the *Scream* trilogy of horror films, drew upon his background as a soap fan (*One Life to Live, All My Children,* and *General Hospital*) when he was creating the prime-time teen serial *Dawson's Creek*.

Six Feet Under star Matthew St. Patrick used to watch the whole ABC lineup. While he never appeared on *One Life to Live,* he did work on either side of it with roles on *AMC* and *GH*.

When *Shark* star Sam Page was working on *All My Children,* he would drive his cast mates crazy, coming in talking about what a great show *One Life to Live* was.

Several of *All My Children*'s cast, past and present, were fans of their sister soap. Mark Consuelos (Mateo Santos), who was born in Spain, learned to speak English watching the ABC soaps with his mother. One day, overwhelmed by all the crying and suffering on the TV, Consuelos asked his mother, "What's the name of this show?" When she told him *One Life to Live,* he responded, "That's not a life I want to live."

Julia Barr had been a soap opera fan before she began her twenty-plus-year run as *AMC*'s Brooke English. In the 1980s, when asked by *Soap Opera Digest* which soap actor from another show she would most like to work with, she responded Roscoe Born, whose performance as Mitch Laurence had captivated her. Years later, Barr's wish came true when Born joined *All My Children* as Brooke's new love interest, child pornographer Jim Thomasen, a character maybe even sleazier than Mitch himself.

Roseanne named the setting of her eponymous TV sitcom Lanford after Llanview.

When Linda Dano appeared on *The Rosie O'Donnell Show,* promoting her four-soap-opera stint, ABC soap fan O'Donnell told Dano that she would be willing to resurrect her *All My Children* character of Naomi on all four soaps, including *One Life to Live.* Although that never materialized, O'Donnell interviewed several *OLTL* cast members, such as Erika Slezak and Robert S. Woods, on her talk show, often giving them first guest honor.

Calvert DeForest, best known to David Letterman fans as Larry "Bud" Melman, never guested on the show, but he did sub for Thom Christopher (Carlo Hesser) during a rehearsal scene. While DeForest was visiting the set, the director asked him if he'd like to run Carlo's lines with Audrey Landers (Charlotte Hesser), who got a kick out of DeForest's interpretation of the usually menacing Carlo Hesser.

Debra Jo Rupp, who played the mother on *That '70s Show,* began her career with a short-term stint on *All My Children* and has remained a fan of the entire ABC afternoon lineup.

Hockey legend Wayne Gretzky might have guested on *One Life to Live* if he hadn't had his fill of acting during a one-day stint as a mobster on his other favorite soap, *The Young and the Restless.* Gretzky does, however, count Robert S. Woods (Bo Buchanan) and Michael Storm (Larry Wolek) among his friends; he has frequently invited them to his celebrity golf tournaments.

The late singer Luther Vandross loved the entire ABC lineup, but considered *One Life to Live* his favorite. He especially loved when he'd hear one of his songs playing in the background of a scene. Although he always wanted to appear on *OLTL*, he did not want to come on as himself and sing a song or two; he wanted to play a gangster.

Richard Burton, considered one of the best actors in the history of stage and film, could not watch *One Life to Live* religiously. The show was not carried in England where he was living. Whenever he was working in New York, however, he made sure to catch up on the goings-on in Llanview.[56]

Dream Come True

In the late eighties, country music superstar and *One Life to Live* fan Reba McEntire stopped by the studio. When she saw Andrea Evans, she couldn't resist giving "Tina" a hug. In the nineties, McEntire returned to the studio to perform on the show. In the context of the story line, it was revealed that Reba was a longtime friend of Luna Moody, and Reba later performed at the bar Rodi's. As a gift to thank the show for having her on, McEntire offered cast and crew tickets to her concert at Radio City Music Hall. A few years later, ABC tapped McEntire to host its miniseries *A Daytime to Remember,* introducing classic episodes of the ABC soaps.

In addition to promoting her new CD, soul diva Mary J. Blige performed at Antonio Vega's club Capricorn because she had been watching the show since she was a little girl. While on the set, she would point to actors such as Kassie DePaiva and tell them, "I know you. I know who you are." Blige, it should be noted, did not perform her hit "No More

Drama," which mixed in theme music from *The Young and the Restless*.

Famed trumpeter Chris Botti, who performed at Club Indigo and flirted on-screen with Kelly Cramer (Gina Tognoni), performed his trumpet exercises in college while watching *One Life to Live*.

Horror novelist Peter Straub (*Ghost Story, Shadowland*) played the blind ex–police detective who filled in John McBain (Michael Easton) about the circumstances surrounding his father's death. While on the set, Straub struck up a friendship with Easton, himself a writer and poet. The two have collaborated on a comic book, *The Tales of the Green Woman*.

Singer Darlene Love, who performed on the show with Righteous Brother Bill Medley, had been a regular fan of the show and loved it, but was shocked one day to walk in and discover her father watching. Even though he'd been caught, he denied that he was a soap fan.

Rap music pioneer Kurtis Blow not only performed during the rap story line of the early nineties, he also served as a consultant—a job he landed because of his being a fan. A friend of Blow's who was working as a stagehand on the show arranged for Blow to come and meet some of the cast members, get their autographs. While on set, Blow heard about the plans for an upcoming rap story line. One of the directors told him that they would need some input from a rap music professional to make sure that the story line remained true. The story line, in which Kerry Nichols dropped out of college to pursue a career in rap music, reminded Blow of his own history.

Tony Award winner Phyllis Newman (*Subways Are for Sleeping*) originated the role of Renee Divine, an ex-madam and the love of Asa Buchanan's life. A fan of the show, she loved getting the chance to kiss Asa, which also provided her with the first romantic kissing scene she'd done in years. When the producers opted to keep Renee around, Newman wanted to stay, but she had already accepted a role on a prime-time series, *Coming of Age*.

So devoted was Sammy Davis, Jr., to his soaps that he would bring a portable TV set with him to afternoon rehearsals. He became one of the first celebrities to use his fame to work on the shows he loved. In the mid-seventies, he sang on the CBS classic *Love of Life*. In the early eighties, he played a dying actor desperate to reconnect with his estranged son on *General Hospital*. Daytime fans, however, remember him best for his stints on *One Life to Live*. Davis had been watching the show for six years when he came on the show in 1980 for a week of guest appearances, playing eyepatched con artist Chip Warren. He enjoyed himself so much that he came back for a second run. His work on the show earned him a 1980 Daytime Emmy nomination for Best Cameo.

They Were Fans First

Some actors, like Erika Slezak (Viki Lord Davidson), began their lives in Llanview without ever having watched a soap opera before. Others were fans of a different show; Robert S. Woods (Bo Buchanan) got hooked on *Guiding Light* while waiting for *All in the Family* reruns. Then there is the select group of actors, like Valarie Pettiford (Sheila Price), who show up on the set as familiar with Llanview as with their own hometowns.

Catherine Hickland had been watching *One Life to Live* for eighteen years by the time she was hired to play Lindsay Rappaport. Her favorite story line was Megan's death. She has likened working on the show alongside favorites Erika Slezak (Viki Lord Davidson) and Hillary B. Smith (Nora Buchanan) to one of those dreams where you suddenly are on a show you watch.[57]

Barbara Treutelaar, who came on as Didi O'Neill, a love interest for Bo Buchanan, in the mid-eighties, had been watching the show since the very first episode.

Although Kassie DePaiva (Blair Cramer) had already

worked on a soap opera, *Guiding Light,* for several years, she was nervous her first week at *One Life to Live.* In her first scenes, she was working with Erika Slezak (Viki Lord Davidson), whom she had grown up watching.

Like DePaiva, Crystal Chappell (Maggie Carpenter) had always idolized the work of Erika Slezak. She hated when *One Life* veered away from its focus on the Lords and the Buchanans. When Chappell finally joined the show, she literally froze when she spotted Slezak on the set, wanting to go up and speak but afraid to do so.

James DePaiva (Max Holden) had long been a fan of the show before he came to New York looking to break in to daytime. He really wanted to work on *One Life to Live*—so much so that when he auditioned for other shows like *Another World,* it just didn't feel right.

When Brynn Thayer's agent called to tell her about the audition for the role of Jenny Wolek, Thayer was more than a little nervous. Since college, she had been a devoted soap opera fan. She never took classes that would conflict with *Love Is a Many Splendored Thing* or *All My Children.* By the time she was living in New York, she had become a fan of *One Life to Live* as well. So she was not only familiar with Katherine Glass, the actress she would be replacing, she loved Glass in the role and hated to see her leave.[58]

Like Thayer, Marva Hicks (Jacara Principal) scheduled her classes around her soap opera schedule of *All My Children* and *One Life to Live.*

Sandra P. Grant (Rachel Gannon) first started watching during Judith Light's run as Karen Wolek.

Chris Beetem (Tate Harmon) had become a fan of the

Robin Strasser (left) almost turned down the role of Dorian Lord because she worried that the role had no future. Also pictured: Erika Slezak (right), who plays Viki Lord Davidson.

show while tuning in to watch his good friend Nathaniel Marston (Al Holden and Dr. Michael McBain).

Being a fan nearly kept Robin Strasser from joining the cast. When the producers first approached her about taking over the role of Dorian Lord, she was hesitant. She had been watching the day that Dorian killed her husband Victor Lord and didn't see a long future for the character.[59] The producers assured her she didn't have to worry about that.

John McBain's Ten Most Wanted List

In the five years since Michael Easton joined the show as John McBain, the character has been fighting crime as an FBI agent, as part of the Llanview police department, and even on his own without a badge. While most cops try not to make their cases personal, that, as John has learned the hard way, proves nearly impossible to do while investigating your own father's murder and when serial killers target your lovers.

1. Flynn Laurence
   When the audience first met John McBain, he easily could have been mistaken for one of the bad guys, working for a Las Vegas mobster by the name of Flynn Laurence. As it turned out, John was an FBI agent working undercover to bust up Flynn's crime ring. When Natalie Buchanan refused to throw a pool game, Flynn had her kidnapped, forcing John to blow his cover and rescue the woman with whom he would fall in love. Flynn, it should be noted, would not be the

last criminal from whom John would need to rescue
Natalie.

2. Dr. Stephen Haver (a/k/a The Music Box Killer)
   An unsolved murder case came back to haunt John.
   The Music Box Killer, the same strangler who had
   killed John's fiancée Caitlin Fitzgerald, set about
   killing women in Llanview, among them Police Commissioner Bo Buchanan's fiancée Gabrielle Medina. Dr.
   Haver, a psychiatrist, was not only bold enough to
   target the women his pursuers loved, he was bold
   enough to work alongside them, providing input on the
   killer's psychological profile.

3. The Santi Crime Family
   The Santi Crime Family, headed up by Tico Santi,
   murdered Kathryn Fitzgerald, who was not only a
   colleague of John's from the FBI but the sister of his
   murdered fiancée. (Like so many women in John's life,
   she also carried a torch for him.) When Natalie Buchanan's presumed dead husband Cristian Vega killed
   Tico Santi, he helped John out on both the work and
   home fronts: Cristian not only closed the case for
   John, his subsequent imprisonment eliminated him as
   a rival for Natalie's heart.

4. RJ Gannon
   Although RJ Gannon was usually involved in some sort
   of illegal operation, he targeted John McBain for purely
   personal reasons. Evangeline Williamson, an attorney,
   dumped RJ for the more law-abiding John, who had

presumably given up on Natalie. Having grown used to people doing his dirty work for him, the brokenhearted RJ hired thugs to rough John up.

5–6. Hayes Barber and Nick Messina (a/k/a The Killing Club Murderers)

Two killers for the price of one. When a serial killer began copying murders from Marcie Walsh's mystery novel, *The Killing Club,* John was already personally invested in the case. Marcie was dating John's brother, Dr. Michael McBain. Double the killers meant double the danger for the women in John's life. Barber and Messina kidnapped not one but two of John's women: Evangeline Williamson, who had just broken up with him, and Natalie Buchanan, for whom he still pined. Once again, John had to rescue Natalie, which brought them back together.

7.   Carlo Hesser

John McBain finally got to tangle with Llanview's most notorious mobster, Carlo Hesser. While John was visiting Cristian Vega in Statesville prison, Carlo started a riot that trapped John inside.

8–9. David Vickers and Spencer Truman

John's investigation into the murder of his father, a police officer, led him to uncover a mystery involving con artist David Vickers and his presumably respectable brother, Dr. Spencer Truman. While it originally looked as though David Vickers had shot John's father, the discovery of the murder weapon revealed that the not-so-good Dr. Truman was the real shooter. When Dr. Truman was stabbed to death, John was a natural suspect. Even Natalie, who was then training with the forensics team, hid evidence that she feared would link John to the murder. After confessions from his one-time nemesis David Vickers and later from his new love interest Marty Saybrooke, John finally arrested the real murderess, Lindsay Rappaport.

10. Marcie Walsh McBain
John spent the final quarter of 2007 tracking down his sister-in-law Marcie, who had fled town with Todd Manning's son after losing custody of the boy. John was tracking Marcie down unofficially, as he had lost his badge after the revelation that he had known that his adopted nephew Tommy was actually Todd Manning's presumed dead son.

Vega-Bonds

It was not until well into their adult lives that Antonio and Cristian Vega discovered they were not biological brothers but cousins. Although Carlotta Vega had raised Antonio as her son, she was actually his aunt; her brother, his father, Manuel Santi, had been a crime lord in Puerto Rico. While Antonio was shaken by the news of his true paternity, the revelation has not been able to sever the fraternal bond between himself and Cristian. They continue to watch out for each other. Cristian won't, for instance, kill Antonio—even when he's been brainwashed into doing so. Antonio and Cristian also continue to share all those same things brothers do . . .

Women

Jessica Buchanan. The Buchanan heiress dated Cristian in her teens and later married Antonio. She also cheated on both brothers. After putting Cristian off for months, the then-virginal Jessica got drunk one night and slept with Will Rappaport. Years later, Jessica took up with Antonio (by which time Cristian had moved on to Jessica's own sister Natalie).

Jessica cheated on Antonio with Nash Brennan when her alternate personality, Tess, emerged. Antonio married Jessica despite Tess's "infidelity"—and the fact that she had given birth to Nash's baby. (Years earlier, the equally noble Cristian had offered to raise as his own the baby Jessica conceived with Will.) Jessica eventually cheated on Antonio with Nash, an affair she could not blame this time on mental illness.

Roseanne Delgado. Jessica was not the first woman who went from Cristian to Antonio. Still reeling from Jessica's relationship with Will, Cristian jumped into a hasty marriage with the scheming Roseanne Delgado. After the marriage was annulled, Roseanne took up with Antonio, who hadn't learned from his brother's mistake. Roseanne sabotaged her relationship when she spied on the police department for criminal RJ Gannon and intentionally withheld information that nearly got Antonio's female partner killed. Antonio finally understood what his brother *didn't see* in Roseanne.

A Prison Record

Cristian entered Statesville Prison as a legacy inmate thanks to older brother Antonio.

When the Vega family was introduced, Antonio was off-screen, serving time at Statesville for murder. Justifiable homicide, it turned out. He had killed in self-defense. His record was eventually cleaned up shiny enough that he could earn a law degree and join the police department.

Years later, Cristian would also go to Statesville on a murder rap. As with his older brother, there were mitigating circumstances. Cristian had been programmed into killing Antonio's mobster brother Tico.

The Vega brothers, it should be noted, made a very

effective tag-team in the death of Tico Santi: Antonio shot his brother in the line of duty; then a brainwashed Cristian pulled the plug on his comatose cousin. Of course, Antonio was accused of the crime, but aren't big brothers supposed to cover for their younger siblings?

Mutual Enemies

Carlo Hesser. Llanview's own kingpin of crime turned out to be the mastermind behind turning Cristian into a killing machine. Years earlier, Carlo had tried to manipulate Antonio, forcing him to repay a hefty loan as the crime lord's right-hand man. Antonio turned the tables and worked undercover with the police to bring Carlo down.

RJ Gannon. When RJ Gannon realized that Cristian had been working undercover with the police to expose his operation, he hired a hit man to rub him out. Although RJ's criminal dealings have put him into conflict with Antonio, the police officer, the main trouble between the men has been personal. Antonio fell in love with RJ's daughter Keri. After she died, RJ schemed for custody of Keri and Antonio's daughter, Jamie.

Clothes *(or lack thereof)*

While most brothers tend to swap clothes, the Vegas tend to share a penchant for getting caught without theirs. When Lindsay Rappaport objected to Cristian dating her daughter, Jen, she hired a computer expert to install a webcam in Cristian's apartment and broadcast his private and often undressed moments on the Internet. Equally embarrassing, one of Antonio's undercover assignments forced him to work as a male stripper.

7
And the Emmy Goes To . . .

The Daytime Emmy Awards

<hr/>

One Life to Live was one of the very first soap operas of its era to be recognized with a Daytime Emmy nomination and the very last of its generation to win that top honor. At the 1973 Emmy Awards, only two soap operas were nominated for Outstanding Program Achievement in Daytime Drama: *One Life to Live* and *The Edge of Night* (which won). Despite its early recognition, *One Life to Live* would not be named Best Daytime Drama for another twenty-nine years.

The 1973 Emmys also presented an award for individual achievement on daytime for the first time. *One Life* director David Pressman was nominated for Outstanding Achievement by an Individual in Daytime Drama, a hodgepodge of a category that also included three other directors, two actors, a scenic designer, and a set decorator. The award ultimately went to Mary Fickett (Ruth Martin, *All My Children*).

In 1974, the Daytime Emmy Awards broke off into their own separate ceremony, allowing for a greater number of categories. Actors no longer needed to compete with directors and set designers. Actors didn't even have to compete against actresses. That first Daytime Emmy ceremony awarded one trophy to *One Life to Live,* Outstanding Technical Direction and Electronic Camera Work—the only Emmy for which it had been nominated. The show did even worse the following year, nominated for absolutely nothing.

While some years (1991, 1997) have proven equally dry for *OLTL*, the show has racked up an impressive number of nominations and awards. One-third of all the Best Actress Emmys have been presented to *One Life to Live*—and the lion's share of those to Erika Slezak (Viki Lord Davidson). Slezak's husband Brian Davies now jokes that their house looks as though Mary Tyler Moore lives there.[60] With six trophies, Slezak holds the record for most Daytime Emmy Awards for playing one role (or in her case seven roles rolled into one). Her former cast mate Al Freeman, Jr. (Captain Ed Hall) holds an important distinction as well, the first African-American soap actor to win a Daytime Emmy.

And now, a year-by-year account of the winners, nominees, curiosities, and the occasional scandal.

1976 Daytime Emmy Awards
Presented May 11, 1976.

- David Pressman, who had lost to *All My Children*'s Mary Fickett, was pitted against only other directors this year and walked away with the Daytime Emmy.
- Shepperd Strudwick, who played Victor Lord, became the first actor from the show to be Emmy-nominated.

1977 Daytime Emmy Awards
Presented May 12, 1977.

- Movie star Farley Granger (*Strangers on a Train, They Live by Night*), who had recently joined the cast as psychiatrist Will Vernon and would soon be leaving, was nominated as Best Actor.
- Gillian Spencer, who originated the role of Victoria Lord Riley, earned her first nomination, not as an actress but as part of the writing team at *As the World Turns,* where she had worked on-screen after leaving *One Life.*

The 1978 Daytime Emmy Awards
Presented June 7, 1978.

- Jennifer Harmon, the final actress to play the emotionally troubled Cathy Craig, earned the first nomination for an actress on *One Life to Live.*
- Dr. Larry Wolek's difficult marriage to Karen earned Michael Storm his first and only Daytime Emmy nomination.

The 1979 Daytime Emmy Awards
Presented May 17, 1979.

- Best Actor Al Freeman, Jr. (Ed Hall) became the first African-American actor to win a Daytime Emmy. He was also nominated later this same year for a (Primetime) Emmy for his work in *Roots: The Next Generation.* That he lost to his *Roots* cast mate Marlon Brando.

The 1980 Daytime Emmy Awards
Presented June 2 and June 4, 1980.

- Karen Wolek's courtroom confession to being a prostitute earned Judith Light the first Best Actress Emmy presented to an actress from *One Life to Live*.
- Karen's scenes also earned the first nomination for the show's writing team, headed up by Gordon Russell and Sam Hall.
- Because of the proliferation of celebrities guesting on daytime, the Academy introduced the category Outstanding Guest/Cameo Appearance. Although the trend would continue, the category disappeared the next year. Sammy Davis, Jr.'s turn as con artist Chip Warren earned him a Cameo nomination.
- Shepperd Strudwick, who had previously been nominated as Best Actor for playing Victor Lord, earned a second nomination, this in the Best Supporting Actor category for playing a college professor on *Love of Life*. That nomination made Strudwick the first actor to be Daytime Emmy–nominated for playing roles on two different shows.

The 1981 Daytime Emmy Awards
Presented May 19 and 21, 1981.

- Not only did Judith Light repeat her victory, so too did the previous year's Best Actor winner, Douglass Watson from *Another World*—the only time in Daytime history when both the Best Actor and Best Actress won back-to-back Emmys.

- Also competing for Best Actress was Light's cast mate Robin Strasser (Dorian Lord).
- Gordon Russell, who died in January of 1981, received a posthumous nomination for his contribution to the writing team, which also included his successor as head writer Sam Hall.
- David Pressman, who had won one of the very few Daytime Emmys given out to individual directors, shared a nomination for Direction with Peter Miner and Norman Hall.
- For her role in the creation of *One Life to Live* and *All My Children* along with contributions to numerous other soap operas (including *Another World,* whose success proved instrumental to the launching of *One Life*), Agnes Nixon was given a Trustees Award for Special Achievement in Television.

The 1982 Daytime Emmy Awards
Presented June 8, 1982.

- Robin Strasser (Dorian Lord) kept *One Life*'s Best Actress streak going, snagging the Emmy for herself.
- Gerald Anthony (Marco Dane) earned his first nomination for Best Supporting Actor.
- David Pressman, Peter Miner, and Norman Hall were again nominated for Outstanding Direction.
- Sam Hall, Peggy O'Shea, and crew picked up a nomination for Outstanding Writing.

The 1983 Daytime Emmy Awards

Presented June 6, 1983.

One Life to Live's numerous nominations this year were part of an ABC domination that prompted NBC, whose turn it was to broadcast the awards, to let them go unaired.

- Erika Slezak (Viki Lord Davidson) was nominated for the first time and really wanted to win to publicly thank for his support her father, Walter Slezak, who had recently died.[61] Also nominated was the previous year's winner and Slezak's on-screen nemesis Robin Strasser (Dorian Lord).
- Although *One Life* did not walk away with a Best Actress Emmy this year, Robert S. Woods (Bo Buchanan) was named Best Actor.
- The show's previous Best Actor winner, Al Freeman, Jr. (Ed Hall) was nominated again, albeit in the Supporting Actor category this time, alongside Best Actress nominee Robin Strasser's leading man Anthony Call (Herb Callison).
- Brynn Thayer earned her sole Best Supporting Actress nomination for the story line in which Jenny Jannsen gave her daughter back to her biological mother.
- Allen Fristoe, whose wife Mary Fickett had beaten David Pressman for that first Emmy, joined the directing team and turned out to be the good luck charm it needed. Fristoe, along with Pressman, Norman Hall, and Peter Miner, won the Emmy for Outstanding Direction.
- The writing team, headed now by Sam Hall, Peggy O'Shea, and S. Michael Schnessel, was also nominated.

The 1984 Daytime Emmy Awards
Presented June 27, 1984.

• The *New York Post,* which had been given a list of winners before the evening ceremony began, published those names in its afternoon edition.

• Erika Slezak (Viki Lord Davidson) won her first Best Actress award. Although she had not intended to, she thanked her husband.[62] Justin Deas, who currently ties Slezak's record for Emmy wins, also won his first this year.

• Anthony Call (Herb Callison) received his second nomination for Best Supporting Actor.

• Christine Ebersole's comic turn as Maxie McDermott earned her a Best Supporting Actress nomination.

• The Outstanding Direction award was given to Larry Auerbach, George Keatherly, Peter Miner, and David Pressman.

The 1985 Daytime Emmy Awards
Presented August 1, 1985.

• Best Actress nominee Robin Strasser (Dorian Lord) competed against the original Viki, Gillian Spencer (now Daisy Cortlandt on *All My Children*), but they lost to Kim Zimmer, who had joined *Guiding Light* after being let go from *One Life* as Echo DiSavoy.

• Compared with Susan Lucci's losing streak, which was picking up media attention, nobody aside from Anthony Call himself took much notice of his third consecutive Best Supporting Actor nomination without a trophy.

• Nominated for Best Direction: David Pressman, Peter

Miner, Larry Auerbach, Melvin Bernhardt, John Sedwick, Ron Lagomarsino, Susan Pomerantz, and Stuart Silver.

The 1986 Daytime Emmy Awards
Presented July 17, 1986.

• As noted in the "40 Years to *Life*" time line, Uta Hagen's nomination as Best Supporting Actress was highly criticized.
• Appropriately enough, Viki's second personality, Niki Smith, helped Erika Slezak win her second Best Actress Emmy.
• A dual role also gave Best Actor David Canary (twins Adam and Stuart Chandler, *All My Children*) the edge over fellow nominee Robert S. Woods.
• Al Freeman, Jr. (Ed Hall) received his third Daytime Emmy nomination, his second as Best Supporting Actor.
• Nominated for Outstanding Direction: Larry Auerbach, Peter Miner, David Pressman, Susan Pomerantz, and Stuart Silver.

The 1987 Daytime Emmy Awards
Presented June 30, 1987.

• After the controversy surrounding Uta Hagen's nomination, the Academy introduced the new category, Outstanding Guest Performer. Like the Outstanding Cameo Appearance category that debuted in 1980, the Outstanding Guest Performer Emmy was only presented one year. Oscar winner Eileen Heckart (*Butterflies Are*

Free), who had previously been nominated for two single performance Emmys for guest spots on *The Mary Tyler Moore Show*, was nominated for her *OLTL* stint as Ruth Perkins.

- Best Supporting Actor nominees Anthony Call (Herb Callison) and Al Freeman, Jr. (Ed Hall) each received their fourth Daytime Emmy nomination.
- Nominated for Outstanding Writing was the team headed by Peggy O'Shea and S. Michael Schnessel.

The 1988 Daytime Emmy Awards
Presented June 29, 1988.

- Many people questioned the inclusion of Andrea Evans (Tina Lord) in the Ingenue category, for which she was nominated. Evans had played the teenager/ingenue when she debuted on the show ten years before.
- Erika Slezak told *Soap Opera Digest* that she suspected that she would be winning this year, but the Outstanding Lead Actress Emmy went to Helen Gallagher (Maeve Ryan, *Ryan's Hope*), who would eventually turn up in Llanview as sex therapist Dr. Maud.
- Nominated for Outstanding Direction: Larry Auerbach, Peter Miner, Gary Bowen, David Pressman, Susan Pomerantz, Lisa Smith Hesser, and Andrea Giles Rich.

The 1989 Daytime Emmy Awards
Presented June 29, 1989.

- Before Linda Dano (Rae Cummings) was nominated for her soap work, she was nominated in the category

Outstanding Talk/Service Show Host for the cable show *Attitudes*.

- Nominated for Outstanding Direction: Larry Auerbach, Peter Miner, Gary Bowen, David Pressman, Jim Sayegh, and Andrea Giles Rich.

The 1990 Daytime Emmy Awards
Presented June 28, 1990.

- S. Michael Schnessel and crew earned the show's lone nomination, Outstanding Writing.

The 1991 Daytime Emmy Awards
Presented June 27, 1991.
For the first time in the history of the Daytime Emmys, the awards ceremony was broadcast in prime time. Unfortunately, that meant nothing to *One Life to Live,* which had been completely shut out of the nominations.

The 1992 Daytime Emmy Awards
Presented June 23, 1992.

- The fact that Susan Lucci was cohosting the ceremony made many people feel that her thirteenth nomination would prove lucky, but it didn't. Erika Slezak won her third Emmy as Viki Lord Davidson. After the audience gave Lucci a standing ovation, she responded by admitting that she herself had voted for Slezak.
- Among the other actresses nominated was Slezak's on-screen daughter Jessica Tuck (Megan Gordon), who had played out an emotional death scene.

- When Thom Christopher (Carlo Hesser) won the Best Supporting Actor Emmy, Jerry ver Dorn's (Clint Buchanan) children teased him that he (ver Dorn) had been beaten by a bald man.[63] (Ver Dorn, who would eventually win back-to-back Best Supporting Actor Emmys, had been nominated for his work on *Guiding Light*.)

- Megan's death not only earned an Emmy for Slezak and a nomination for Tuck, it also earned a nomination for Michael Malone and Josh Griffith, who had been head-writing the show for less than a year at this point. (The nomination was shared with Margaret DePriest and Craig Carlson, who had preceded Malone and Griffith as head writers.)

The 1993 Daytime Emmy Awards
Presented May 26, 1993.

- Gerald Anthony, who had been nominated in 1982 as Best Supporting Actor for playing Marco Dane on *One Life to Live*, won the award for playing the same character on *General Hospital*—an Emmy first.

- Another Emmy first . . . Also nominated for Best Supporting Actor this year was the previous year's winner Thom Christopher. Christopher, who had won for playing gangster Carlo Hesser, was nominated this year as Carlo's twin brother Mortimer. While many actors have been nominated and won Emmys for playing twins, Christopher was the first to be nominated separately for each twin.

- Outstanding Lead Actor David Canary's performance as twins Adam and Stuart Chandler on *All My Children*

again gave him the edge over Robert S. Woods (Bo
Buchanan).

- Tonja Walker's (Alex Olanov) contribution to the story
  line that transformed Mortimer Bern into Carlo Hesser
  earned her a Best Supporting Actress nomination.

The 1994 Daytime Emmy Awards

Presented May 25, 1994.

While never nominated for a Daytime Emmy, James De-
Paiva (Max Holden) did cohost this year's ceremony, with
Susan Lucci, Drake Hogestyn (John Black, *Days of Our
Lives*), and Peter Bergman (Jack Abbott, *The Young and
the Restless*). The major Emmys were, for the most part,
split between *One Life to Live* and *Guiding Light*. The big
award of the night, Outstanding Drama, would have broken the tie except that it went to *All My Children*.

- The gang rape and subsequent trial earned Emmys for
  all the principals involved, including Michael Malone
  and Josh Griffith's writing team. Susan Haskell (Marty
  Saybrooke) was named Best Supporting Actress and
  Roger Howarth (Todd Manning) Best Younger Actor.
- Hillary B. Smith, who played Todd's morally conflicted
  defense attorney, Nora Hanen, won Best Actress.
  Celebrating a birthday that day, Smith declared the
  Emmy "the best birthday present I ever got."
- Best Actor nominee Robert S. Woods (Bo Buchanan)
  lost to former (and future) cast mate Michael Zaslow,
  then Roger Thorpe on *Guiding Light*.
- Thom Christopher was not only Emmy nominated for
  the third time in as many years, he was nominated for a

third role, but this one not on *One Life to Live*. He was nominated for his work on *Loving*.

The 1995 Daytime Emmy Awards
Presented May 20, 1995.

- Erika Slezak won the Best Actress Emmy, her fourth, which set a new record for actresses.
- Too old now—and too villainous, some said—for the Younger Actor category, Roger Howarth (Todd Manning) stepped up into the Supporting Actor category, which was won by Jerry ver Dorn (now Clint Buchanan) for his work on *Guiding Light*.
- A nomination for Outstanding Direction went to the team of Tracy Casper, Jamie Howarth, Tracy Lang, James McDonald, Peter Miner, Jill Mitwell, David Pressman, Lonny Price, Mary Rodden, Jim Sayegh, Gary Tomlin, Frank Valentini, and Stan Warnow.
- Michael Malone and Josh Griffith racked up another nomination for Outstanding Writing.

The 1996 Daytime Emmy Awards
Presented May 16, 1996.
For the first time, fans were allowed to buy tickets to the event, which was held at Radio City Music Hall.

- The ardent fans, many of them rooting for Susan Lucci to finally win, were chanting "Lucci" during Best Actress Erika Slezak's acceptance speech. Slezak won her fifth Emmy, breaking her own record and upsetting *TV Guide*'s prediction that this was Lucci's year.

Viki's alternate personality Niki Smith may have cost Viki Lord Davidson a couple of husbands, but she's helped Erika Slezak win more than a couple of Emmys. Top, Viki (Erika Slezak) in Niki mode; bottom, Viki between husbands—half-brothers Clint Buchanan (then Clint Ritchie) and Ben Davidson (Mark Derwin).

- Nathan Fillion (Joey Buchanan) was nominated as Outstanding Younger Actor.
- Michael Malone and Josh Griffith picked up yet another nomination for writing.

The 1997 Daytime Emmy Awards
Presented May 21, 1997.
One Life to Live was completely shut out of the nominations.

The 1998 Daytime Emmy Awards
Presented May 15, 1998.
While not shut out again, the show picked up one lone nomination, in a technical category, Technical Direction.

The 1999 Daytime Emmy Awards
Presented May 21, 1999.
Once again, *One Life* only earned one nomination, but at least this came in an acting category.

- 1983 Best Actor Robert S. Woods (Bo Buchanan) was nominated alongside all previous winners: Peter Bergman (Jack Abbott, *The Young and the Restless*); Eric Braeden (Victor Newman, *The Young and the Restless*); David Canary (Adam Chandler, *All My Children*)—and Tony Geary (Luke Spencer, *General Hospital*), who won.

The 2000 Daytime Emmy Awards
Presented May 19, 2000.

- For the second year in a row, the same names were nominated for Best Actor: Peter Bergman, Eric

Braeden, David Canary, Tony Geary, and Robert S. Woods. And for the second year in a row, Woods lost to Tony Geary.

- Woods's onetime leading lady Hillary B. Smith (Nora Hanen) was nominated for the first time since her victory in 1994. Perhaps had the awards been presented six days later, on her birthday, she would have walked away with another trophy.
- With a Younger Actress nod for Erin Torpey (Jessica Buchanan) and a Supporting Actor nomination for Timothy Gibbs (Kevin Buchanan), all of Viki's children had been nominated for an Emmy. (Jessica Tuck [Megan Gordon] had been nominated as Best Actress in 1992 and Nathan Fillion [Joey Buchanan] in 1996. At this point in time, neither Viki nor the audience knew about Natalie [Melissa Archer].)
- The show was nominated as Best Drama.

The 2001 Daytime Emmy Awards
Presented May 18, 2001.
The show picked up a pair of technical awards (for Technical Direction and Tape Sound Mixing) along with a handful of technical nominations: Art Direction, Costume Design, Hairstyling, Makeup, and Multi-Camera Editing. The show was not, however, recognized in any of the acting, writing, or directing categories.

The 2002 Daytime Emmy Awards
Presented May 17, 2002.
One Life to Live was finally named Best Drama—a victory

lessened, perhaps, only by the show's failure to capture the two Special Fan Awards for which it had been nominated: Antonio and Keri (Kamar de los Reyes and Sherri Saum) as Favorite Couple and Todd Manning (Roger Howarth) as Favorite Villain.

- A nomination for Best Writing went to the team headed by Lorraine Broderick, who had already won five Emmys as part of the writing teams on *All My Children* and *Guiding Light*.

The 2003 Daytime Emmy Awards
Presented May 17, 2003.

- Linda Dano's (Rae Cummings) nomination for Best Supporting Actress placed her in the select group of actors (among them Thom Christopher and Shepperd Strudwick) who have been nominated for work on two different soaps. Prior to coming back to *One Life*, Dano had won one Emmy and been nominated for numerous others for her work on *Another World*.
- Competing against Dano was her on-screen daughter Robin Christopher (Skye Quartermaine). Christopher had originated the role of Skye on *All My Children*, then resurrected it on *One Life to Live* and was now playing it on *General Hospital*, for which she was receiving her first Daytime Emmy nomination.
- *One Life to Live*'s absence from the Best Writing category might not have been so painful had not almost every other soap opera on television been nominated.

The category had swelled to seven nominees from a list of nine soaps, ignoring only *OLTL* and *Days of Our Lives.*

- Ty Treadway, who was balancing his role as Dr. Troy MacIver with hosting duties on SOAPnet's *Soap Talk* earned an Emmy nomination, along with cohost Lisa Rinna, for Outstanding Talk Show Host. He and Rinna would be nominated again in 2005, 2006, and 2007.

The 2004 Daytime Emmy Awards
Presented May 21, 2004.

- Although *One Life* was not nominated for Best Drama, executive producer Frank Valentini did earn a pair of nominations: one as part of the show's directing team, the other for the song "Flash of Light," which he co-wrote with music director Paul Glass.
- Ilene Kristen (Roxy Balsom) and Kathy Brier (Marcie Walsh) competed against each other in the Best Supporting Actress category, but neither won.

The 2005 Daytime Emmy Awards
Presented May 20, 2005.

- The Best Actress category swelled to an unheard-of eight nominees, among them Kassie DePaiva (Blair Cramer), her first nomination, and Erika Slezak (Viki Lord Davidson), who won. The eight nominees were serenaded by Il Divo.
- Kassie DePaiva actually lost twice this evening. Not only was she not named Best Actress, Blair and Todd

failed to accrue enough phone-in votes to be named
Most Irresistible Combination.

- Heather Tom's (Kelly Cramer) nomination as Best
  Supporting Actress not only placed her into the small
  circle of actors nominated for two different soap roles,
  the nomination, her tenth, set the record for actresses
  under the age of thirty. Prior to coming to *One Life*,
  Tom had racked up nine Emmy nominations, including
  two wins, as Victoria Newman on *The Young and the
  Restless*.
- Competing against Tom was cast mate Ilene Kristen
  (Roxy Balsom).

The 2006 Daytime Emmy Awards
Presented April 28, 2006.

- Best Supporting Actress nominee Renee Elise Goldsberry
  (Evangeline Williamson), the show's lone acting nominee, lost to Gina Tognoni (Dinah Marler on *Guiding
  Light*), who had originated the role of Kelly Cramer.
- John Loprieno, who played Cord Roberts for many
  years, earned his first Daytime Emmy nomination, as
  part of the writing team, headed up by Dena Higley.

The 2007 Daytime Emmy Awards
Presented June 14, 2007.
Mario Van Peebles, who had played a small role on the show
in the 1980s, introduced *One Life to Live*'s clips segment.

- Kevin Buchanan became the only role to earn Daytime
  Emmy nominations for two different actors on the

show: Timothy Gibbs had been nominated as Best
Supporting Actor in 2000; Dan Gauthier was nominated as Best Supporting Actor in 2007.

- Heather Tom (Kelly Cramer) was nominated as Best
  Supporting Actress despite the fact that she, along with
  Best Supporting Actor nominee Dan Gauthier (Kevin
  Buchanan), had both been written off the show months
  before the voting. Renee Elise Goldsberry (Evangeline
  Williamson), who was competing against Tom for Best
  Supporting Actress, was still on the show but on her
  way out.

- *One Life to Live* was nominated for Outstanding
  Direction based, in part, on the tense scenes leading up
  to Todd Manning's (Trevor St. John) execution.

Todd Manning's (Trevor St. John) near execution earned *One Life to Live* nominations for
Best Show and Best Direction.

- Critics predicted that the Best Drama award would go to either *One Life to Live* or *The Bold and the Beautiful,* which has never won top honors. In an unexpected twist, the Emmy was tied between the category's other two nominees, *The Young and the Restless* and *Guiding Light.*

Twenty Questions Times Two

40 Questions About One Life to Live's *First 40 Years*

1968. In his years at Llanview Hospital, Dr. Larry Wolek evolved into the catch-all doctor treating everyone for everything, but what was his medical specialty when the show began?

(a) pediatrics (b) proctology (c) plastic surgery (d) psychiatry

1969. What interrupted Viki and Joe Riley's first trip down the aisle?

(a) A fire broke out.

(b) Niki Smith emerged.

(c) Victor Lord suffered a heart attack.

(d) Dorian Lord showed up, claiming to be Joe's first wife.

1970. What was Vince Wolek arrested for transporting over state lines?

(a) alcohol (b) babies (c) cigarettes (d) drugs

1971. While Joe Riley was presumed dead, where did Viki meet Steve Burke, with whom she would fall in love?

(a) Her father hired him to be her bodyguard.

(b) She accidentally ran him down with her car.

(c) He became her new editor at *The Banner.*

(d) She had interviewed him for a story about political corruption.

1972. Police lieutenant Ed Hall was introduced during the investigation into whose murder?

(a) Marcy Wade (b) Dr. Mark Toland (c) Rachel Wilson (d) Victor Lord

1973. What caused the cerebral hemorrhage that killed Meredith Lord?

(a) She was thrown from a horse.

(b) Niki Smith hit her over the head with a statue.

(c) She fell down a flight of stairs while arguing with her father.

(d) She fell while escaping from criminals who had taken her hostage.

1974. Why did Dorian institutionalize her sister Melinda?

(a) Melinda had tried to kill herself.

(b) Melinda tried to kill Dorian and her boyfriend Mark.

(c) Dorian was jealous of Mark's interest in Melinda.

(d) Melinda had become a heroin addict.

1975. Jenny Wolek left Llanview to work in a convent in what South American country?

(a) San Alicia (b) San Bernardo (c) San Carlos (d) San Davio

1976. In what sport was Brad Vernon a pro?

(a) baseball (b) football (c) tennis (d) golf

1977. How were Larry Wolek and Karen Wolek related before they got married?

(a) They were cousins.

(b) Karen was Larry's stepmother.

(c) Karen had been Larry's sister-in-law.

(d) No relation. The last names were mere coincidence.

1978. What sort of show did Pat Ashley host on WVLE?

(a) advice to the lovelorn (b) beauty makeovers (c) cooking

(d) talk show

1979. Who was the first person to realize that Dr. Mario Correlli was in fact his supposedly dead brother Marco Dane?

(a) Karen Wolek (b) Larry Wolek (c) Dorian Lord (d) Edwina Lewis

1980. What secret was Dr. Ivan Kipling willing to kill to protect?

(a) He was a Nazi war criminal.

(b) He frequented prostitutes.

(c) He had never gone to medical school.

(d) He performed experimental surgery on homeless men.

1981. What was the ominous name of the Llanview estate where Asa Buchanan had imprisoned his first wife, Olympia?

(a) Widow's Peak (b) Timberdark (c) Ravenwood (d) Moor Cliffe

1982. What was the name of the alternate energy source Tony Lord and Bo Buchanan sought to mine?

(a) gravitomite (b) buchanium (c) solaramite (d) llanvium

1983. How did Countess Echo DiSavoy earn her unusual nickname?

(a) because of her ability to imitate voices over the telephone

(b) because of her resemblance to her mother

(c) because of her unusually deep singing voice

(d) "Echo" was an acronym for her full name, Eleanor Claire Helena Olivia.

1984. Which of the following was not one of the O'Neill sisters?

(a) Alice (b) Joy (c) Connie (d) Didi

1985. Where did Tina discover the entrance to Victor Lord's secret room?

(a) in the library at Llanfair

(b) in the carriage house

(c) in the basement of *The Banner*

(d) in his mausoleum

1986. On what terrorist-infested island did Cord and Tina Roberts honeymoon after their first wedding?

(a) Angel's Wing (b) Bootlegger's Hideaway (c) Captain's Paradise

(d) Devil's Claw

1987. How was Clint Buchanan blinded?

(a) He was shot in the head.

(b) He developed a brain tumor.

(c) A bomb exploded in his face.

(d) He was trapped in a chemical fire at *The Banner*.

1988. What had Ursula Blackwell rigged to blow up on Tina Lord when she remarried Cord Roberts?

(a) the church (b) the bouquet (c) the wedding cake

(d) the horse-drawn carriage

Cord Roberts (John Loprieno) remarried Tina Lord (Andrea Evans) in a literally explosive double ceremony with Asa Buchanan (Phil Carey) and Renée Divine (Patricia Elliott).

1989. What seasonally named soap actress was Megan Gordon's main competitor for the Daisy Award for Best Actress?

(a) Autumn Days   (b) Spring Skye   (c) Summer Sands   (d) Silver Winters

1990. For what organization was Alex Olanov working when she took over the assignment to find the missing Sarah Buchanan?

(a) FAB (Federal Anticrime Bureau)

(b) ISB (International Security Bureau)

(c) WSB (World Security Bureau)

(d) The Triple I (International Intelligence & Investigation)

1991. Carlo Hesser drugged Viki to bring out Niki Smith for what purpose?

(a) to kill Asa Buchanan

(b) to kill Viki's daughter Megan

(c) to convince Renee to marry him

(d) to burn down *The Banner*

1992. What was the title of the biography Sloan Carpenter wrote about Victor Lord?

(a) *Dark Victor*   (b) *Victorious*   (c) *Citizen Lord*   (d) *Lord of* The Banner

1993. Where did Cassie Callison find a newborn baby on Christmas Eve?

(a) at the mall   (b) under her tree   (c) in the church manger scene
(d) in the backseat of her car

1994. Why was Todd Manning pardoned for his crimes?

(a) Blair Cramer seduced the governor into pardoning him.

(b) Larry Wolek discovered a brain tumor that made Todd not criminally responsible for his crimes.

(c) Todd rescued Marty Saybrooke, CJ Roberts, and Jessica Buchanan from a car accident.

(d) Todd agreed to testify against mob boss Carlo Hesser.

1995. Patrick Thornhart ran afoul of a terrorist organization known as the Men of what number?

(a) 8   (b) 13   (c) 21   (d) 100

1996. What were the names of the two warring gangs in Angel Square?

(a) The Arrows and the Prides

(b) The Bullets and the Hawks

(c) The Cutters and the Wolves

(d) The Diehards and the Falcons

1997. How much money did Todd Manning pay his lawyer Téa Delgado to marry him?

(a) Half a million dollars   (b) $1 million   (c) $5 million   (d) $10 million

1998. Which presumedly dead villain greeted Dorian Lord's host during her trip to Hell?

(a) Mitch Laurence   (b) Marco Dane   (c) Carlo Hesser   (d) Victor Lord

1999. What song did Viki sing during the karaoke contest at the Crossroads Bar?

(a) "Ben"   (b) "I Will Survive"   (c) "Crazy"   (d) "It's Raining Men"

2000. Nora Hanen was presumed to have been killed in what disaster?

(a) car crash   (b) train explosion   (c) plane crash   (d) boating accident

2001. Max Holden interrupted Asa Buchanan's wedding to Gabrielle Medina thinking that Asa was remarrying which of his ex-wives?

(a) Alex   (b) Blair   (c) Becky Lee   (d) Delila

2002. What was the title of the musical Fourth of July episode set in a women's prison?

(a) "Jailhouse Pop"   (b) "Babes Behind Bars"   (c) "Cell Block Party"
(d) "Stars in Stripes"

2003. Al Holden called his disc jockey persona the Voice of What?

(a) Romance   (b) Choice   (c) the Night   (d) Reason

2004. To what political office was Kevin Buchanan elected?

(a) mayor of Llanview   (b) lieutenant governor of Pennsylvania

(c) state senator   (d) district attorney

2005. How did Margaret Cochran blackmail Todd into sleeping with her?

(a) She threatened to kill Blair.

(b) She had kidnapped his children.

(c) She threatened to set fire to the bed to which he was tied.

(d) She threatened to turn evidence against him over to the police.

2006. What natural disaster hit Llanview during Michael and Marcie McBain's wedding?

(a) avalanche   (b) tornado   (c) earthquake   (d) flood

2007. What was the name of the white supremacist organization responsible for arson attacks against minority groups in Llanview?

(a) Last Frontier   (b) The True Masters   (c) One Pure People

(d) The White Right

Answer Key

Twenty Questions Times Two

1968. (d) psychiatry; 1969. (b) Niki Smith emerged; 1970. (d) drugs; 1971. (c) He became her new editor at *The Banner*; 1972. (a) Marcy Wade; 1973. (d) She fell while escaping from criminals who had taken her hostage; 1974. (b) Melinda tried to kill Dorian and her boyfriend Mark; 1975. (c) San Carlos; 1976. (c) tennis; 1977. (a) They were cousins; 1978. (d) talk show; 1979. (a) Karen Wolek; 1980. (b) He frequented prostitutes; 1981. (d) Moor Cliffe; 1982. (c) solaramite; 1983. (b) because of her resemblance to her mother; 1984. (a) Alice; 1985. (a) in the library at Llanfair; 1986. (d) Devil's Claw; 1987. (a) He was shot in the head; 1988. (c) the wedding cake; 1989. (b) Spring Skye; 1990. (a) FAB (Federal Anticrime Bureau); 1991. (b) to kill Viki's daughter Megan; 1992. (d) *Lord of The Banner*; 1993. (c) in the church manger scene; 1994. (c) Todd rescued Marty Saybrooke, CJ Roberts, and Jessica Buchanan from a car accident; 1995. (c) 21; 1996. (a) The Arrows and the Prides; 1997. (c) $5 million; 1998.

(c) Carlo Hesser; 1999. (b) "I Will Survive"; 2000. (b) train explosion; 2001. (a) Alex; 2002. (b) "Babes Behind Bars"; 2003. (c) the Night; 2004. (b) lieutenant governor of Pennsylvania; 2005. (a) She threatened to kill Blair; 2006. (b) tornado; 2007. (c) One Pure People

Notes

1. Robert LaGuardia, *Soap World* (New York: Arbor House, 1983), p. 62.

2. Internet Movie Database, http://www.imdb.com/title/tt0062595/trivia.

3. Jason Bonderoff, "Unforgiven," *Soap Opera Digest*, February 28, 1995, p. 40.

4. Carolyn Hinsey, "Carey On," *Soap Opera Digest*, August 31, 1999, pp. 29–30.

5. Robert Rorke, "From Odyssey House to Heaven: *One Life to Live* Celebrates Twenty Years," *Soap Opera Digest*, July 26, 1988, p. 24.

6. The Official Clint Ritchie Page and Fan Club Headquarters, http://www.clintritchie.com/clints-biography/.

7. "Where Are They Now?," *Soap Opera Digest*, January 19, 1999, p. 45.

8. William Keck, "Gays of Our Lives," *Soap Opera Digest*, December 1, 1998. Reprinted at http://www.geocities.com/hollywood/4616/sod1201d.html.

9. Corrections, *The New York Times*, August 28, 1983, reprinted at http://www.nytimes.com.

10. Sheila Steinbach, "An Exclusive Interview with *OLTL*'s Erika Slezak—After 24 Years, She STILL Loves Viki," *Soap Opera Magazine*, March 14, 1995, reprinted at the Erika Slezak Fan Club Web site, http://www.members.tripod.com/erika_slezak/ESFC/24years.htm.

11. "Labines Bringing New Life to *OLTL*," *Soap Opera Digest*, February 11, 1997, p. 15.

12. "The Latest on *GL*'s Michael Zaslow," *Soap Opera Digest*, September 23, 1997, p. 5.

13. Rorke, p. 24.

14. Debra Nencel, "Phyllis Behar: Her Private Oasis," *Soap Opera Digest*, March 11, 1980, p. 115.

15. Robert A. Waldron, "Triumphant Comebacks!" *Soap Opera Digest*, July 29, 1986, p. 134.

16. Soap Star Stats, *Soap Opera Digest* Web site, http://www.soapoperadigest.com/soapstarstats/breewilliamson bio/.

17. Alison Sloane, " 'The Role from Hell,' " *Soap Opera Digest*, November 24, 1992, p. 119.

18. Michael Logan, "Back on Old Stomping Ground," *Soap Opera Digest*, June 30, 1987, p. 104.

19. Carolyn Hinsey, "Catherine the Great," *Soap Opera Digest*, August 18, 1998, p. 39.

20. Daniel Coleridge, *The Q Guide to Soap Operas* (New York: Alyson Books, 2006), p. 84.

21. "Dancing with the Star," *Soap Opera Digest*, February 27, 2007, p. 19.

22. "Gossip," *Soap Opera Digest*, January 23, 2007, p. 62.

23. Ellen Holly, *One Life: The Autobiography of an*

African American Actress (New York: Kodansha International, 1996), p. 199.

24. "Where Are They Now?," *Soap Opera Digest,* August 8, 1989, p. 89.

25. Rorke, p. 22.

26. Hinsey, "Carey On," p. 30.

27. "Roundup," *Soap Opera Digest,* January 9, 1990, p. 14.

28. "ABC Gossip," *Soap Opera Digest,* June 10, 2003, p. 68.

29. "Four Better . . . Or Worse: Erika Slezak Takes Stock of Viki's Best—and Worst—Storylines," *Soap Opera Digest,* September 23, 1997, p. 64.

30. Mary Beth Sammons, "Sleeping Beauties," *Soap Opera Digest,* December 13, 1988, p. 89.

31. "Mother's Ilk," *Soap Opera Digest,* May 11, 1999, p. 87.

32. "Gossip," *Soap Opera Digest,* May 1, 2007, p. 62.

33. "Roundup," *Soap Opera Digest,* January 1, 1990, p. 13.

34. Robert Rorke, "If I Get Sick, I'm History," *Soap Opera Digest,* September 22, 1997, pp. 37–38.

35. Carolyn Hinsey, "One Life to Leave," *Soap Opera Digest,* February 22, 2000, p. 50.

36. Peter Golden, "Taking the Show on the Road," *Soap Opera Digest,* February 12, 1985, pp. 135–136.

37. Carol Bialkowski, "The Cincinnati Kid," *Soap Opera Digest,* April 28, 1992, p. 131.

38. Rebecca Detken, "Playing by Heart," *Soap Opera Digest,* February 16, 1999, p. 33.

39. Ellen Byron, "Alone Again . . . Naturally," *Soap Opera Digest,* May 17, 1988, p. 113.

40. Michael Small, "Soap Stars Gerry Anthony and Brynn Thayer Have Two Lives to Live, and Live Them Together," *People*, September 6, 1982, reprinted at http://www.geocities .com/historypg/ar820906.html.

41. Alan Carter, "Diamonds Are Forever," *Soap Opera Digest*, April 29, 1997, p. 42.

42. Kristin Gallagher, "Bonita Vanita," *Soap Opera Digest*, September 28, 1998, p. 56.

43. Ellen Byron, "Drama Queen," *Soap Opera Digest*, November 24, 1992, p. 30.

44. Holly, pp. 199–200.

45. The Official Clint Ritchie Page and Fan Club Headquarters, http://www.clintritchie.com/clints-biography/.

46. "ABC Gossip," *Soap Opera Digest*, May 11, 1999, p. 71.

47. Holly, pp. 207–208.

48. "Buchanan Brides," *Soap Opera Digest*, September 23, 1997, p. 67.

49. Jennifer Lenhart, "Decent Proposals," *Soap Opera Digest*, April 29, 2003, p. 42.

50. "Shall We Trance?," *Soap Opera Digest*, September 23, 1997, p. 65.

51. Carolyn Hinsey, "I Object!," *Soap Opera Digest*, August 27, 1996, p. 35.

52. Carolyn Hinsey, "Into the Sunset," *Soap Opera Digest*, December 15, 1998, p. 35.

53. "Roundup," *Soap Opera Digest*, February 6, 2007, p. 56.

54. Randee Dawn, "Out from the Shadows," *Soap Opera Digest*, August 18, 1998, p. 44.

55. Rebecca Dana, "Me Talk Pretty One Daytime," *The New York Observer,* May 14, 2006, reprinted online, http://www.observer.com/node/38844.

56. Seli Groves, "New York News," *Soap Opera Digest,* September 16, 1980, p. 123.

57. "ABC Gossip," *Soap Opera Digest,* August 11, 1998, p. 91.

58. Pam Payne, "The Peacemaker," *Soap Opera Digest,* October 16, 1979, p. 109.

59. Hinsey, "One Life to Leave," p. 51.

60. Kathy Henderson, "Multiplicity," *Soap Opera Digest,* October 8, 1996, p. 32.

61. Henderson, p. 33.

62. Andrea Payne, "Emmy Excitement," *Soap Opera Digest,* September 11, 1984, p. 112.

Bibliography

Books

Coleridge, Daniel. *The Q Guide to Soap Operas.* New York: Alyson Books, 2006.

Holly, Ellen. *One Life: An Autobiography of an African American Actress.* New York: Kodansha America Inc., 1996.

Hyatt, Wesley. *The Encyclopedia of Daytime Television.* New York: Billboard Books, 1997.

LaGuardia, Robert. *Soap World.* New York: Arbor Books, 1983.

Warner, Gary. *One Life to Live: Thirty Years of Memories.* New York: ABC / Daytime Press, 1998.

Periodicals

Bialkowski, Carol. "The Cincinnati Kid." *Soap Opera Digest.* April 28, 1992.

Bonderoff, Jason. "Unforgiven." *Soap Opera Digest.* February 28, 1995.

Byron, Ellen. "Alone Again . . . Naturally." *Soap Opera Digest*. May 17, 1988.

Byron, Ellen. "Drama Queen." *Soap Opera Digest*. November 24, 1992.

Carter, Alan. "Diamonds Are Forever." *Soap Opera Digest*. April 29, 1997.

Dana, Rebecca. "Me Talk Pretty One Daytime." *The New York Observer*. May 14, 2006.

Dawn, Randee. "Out from the Shadows." *Soap Opera Digest*. August 18, 1998.

Detken, Rebecca. "Playing by Heart." *Soap Opera Digest*. February 16, 1999.

Gallagher, Kristin. "Bonita Vanita." *Soap Opera Digest*. September 28, 1998.

Golden, Peter. "Taking the Show on the Road." *Soap Opera Digest*. February 12, 1985.

Henderson, Kathy. "Multiplicity." *Soap Opera Digest*. October 8, 1996.

Hinsey, Carolyn. "I Object!" *Soap Opera Digest*. August 27, 1996.

Hinsey, Carolyn. "Catherine the Great." *Soap Opera Digest*. August 18, 1998.

Hinsey, Carolyn. "Into the Sunset." *Soap Opera Digest*. December 15, 1998.

Hinsey, Carolyn. "Carey On." *Soap Opera Digest*. August 31, 1999.

Hinsey, Carolyn. "One Life to Leave." *Soap Opera Digest*. February 22, 2000.

Holly, Ellen. "How Black Do You Have to Be?" *New York Times*. September 15, 1968.

Holly, Ellen. "Living a White Lie—For a While." *New York Times*. August 10, 1969.

Keck, William. "Gays of Our Lives." *Soap Opera Digest*. December 1, 1998.

Lenhart, Jennifer. "Decent Proposals." *Soap Opera Digest*. April 29, 2003.

Logan, Michael. "On Old Stomping Ground." *Soap Opera Digest*. June 30, 1987.

Nencel, Debra. "Phyllis Behar: Her Private Oasis." *Soap Opera Digest*. March 11, 1980.

Nixon, Agnes. "They're Happy to Be Hooked." *New York Times*. July 7, 1968.

Nixon, Agnes. "What Do the Soaps Have to Do to Win Your Approval?" *New York Times*. May 26, 1972.

Payne, Andrea. "Emmy Excitement." *Soap Opera Digest*. September 11, 1984.

Payne, Pam. "The Peacemaker." *Soap Opera Digest*. October 16, 1979.

Rorke, Robert. "From Odyssey House to Heaven: *One Life to Live* Celebrates Twenty Years." *Soap Opera Digest*. July 26, 1988.

Rorke, Robert. "If I Get Sick, I'm History." *Soap Opera Digest*. September 22, 1997.

Sammons, Mary Beth. "Sleeping Beauties." *Soap Opera Digest*. December 13, 1988.

Sloane, Alison. " 'The Role from Hell.' " *Soap Opera Digest*. November 24, 1992.

Small, Michael. "Soap Stars Gerry Anthony and Brynn Thayer Have Two Lives to Live, and Live Them Together." *People*. September 6, 1982.

Soap Opera Digest. 1979–2007.

Steinbach, Sheila. "An Exclusive Interview with *OLTL*'s Erika Slezak—After 24 Years, She STILL Loves Viki." *Soap Opera Magazine.* March 14, 1995.

Waldron, Robert A. "Triumphant Comebacks!" *Soap Opera Digest.* July 29, 1986.

Web Sites

The Erika Slezak Fan Club Web site
http://www.members.tripod.com/erika_slezak

Internet Movie Database
http://www.imdb.com

Kassie DePaiva's Official Web Site
http://www.kassiedepaiva.com

The Official Clint Ritchie Page and Fan Club Headquarters
http://www.clintritchie.com

Soap Opera Digest Web site
http://www.soapoperadigest.com